Arizona

SCENIC WONDERS *of the* GRAND CANYON STATE

Contents

Introduction   1

7
Grand Canyon Country

27
High Country

44
Indian Country

59
Desert Country

Resources   76
Places to See   Inside back cover
Photo Credits   Inside back flap

This is a land of illusions and thin air. The vision is so cleared at times that the truth itself is deceptive.

—JOHN C. VAN DYKE, *THE DESERT*, 1901

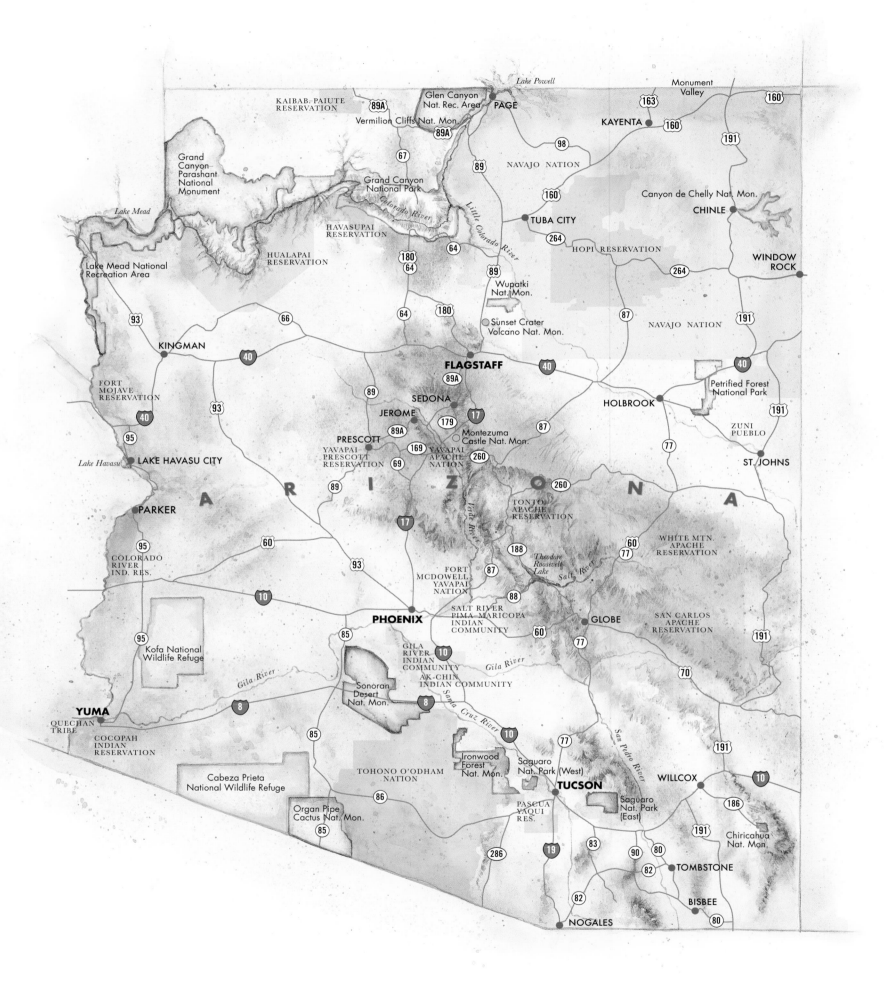

Introduction

Arizona possesses a wealth of scenic beauty. Famous wonders like the Grand Canyon, Lake Powell, and the stately saguaro cactus are only a few of the state's numerous natural and manmade attractions. Although home to three of the nation's largest deserts and inhabited by a wide variety of unique desert animals and plants, Arizona has much more to offer. From Flagstaff's snowcapped peaks to Sedona's striking red rocks, from the panoramic vistas of the Colorado Plateau to the forests of the White Mountains, beauty abounds.

Arizona's human history is just as fascinating as its natural history. Cliff dwellings dramatically perch hundreds of feet above canyon floors, and the ruins of sprawling four-story pueblos recall ancient desert civilizations. Spanish missions testify to the legacy of missionaries who sought to spread Christianity. Former mining boomtowns have been reborn as quirky art communities or living museums of the Wild West, where legendary gunfights are reenacted for tourists and filmmakers.

Even though Phoenix, Arizona's capital, is now the fifth-largest city in the U.S., vast open spaces remain throughout the state. Wilderness areas, wildlife preserves, national parks, and national forests invite exploration and preserve Arizona's breathtaking panoramas and unique wildlife for generations to come.

Geology

Geologists love Arizona because 2 billion years of geological history are showcased in its canyons, mountains, and deserts. Over eons of time, tremendous forces created every type of earthly terrain, from volcanic mountains to oceanside sand dunes. Arizona's lands, lakes, and rivers were formed the same way as the rest of the planet, through plate tectonics, volcanism, faulting, weathering, erosion, and sedimentary deposition.

Paleogeologists believe that millions of years ago the earth's hard crust broke into pieces called tectonic plates, which continue to merge, break up, collide with each other, and pull away again. Earthquakes, volcanic activity, and uplifts occur when tectonic plates overlap or pull apart.

Tectonic actions combined with erosion and deposition to create the mountains, mesas, canyons, and basins seen in Arizona today. Although now almost completely dormant, numerous volcanic fields, along with massive faulting and uplifting, played a major role in the production of Arizona's landforms and abundant mineral deposits.

The state's earliest geologic record can be found in the 1.7-billion-year-old Precambrian rock strata exposed at the bottom of the Grand Canyon. The Precambrian Era consisted of many million-year cycles of sedimentary deposits, mountainous upheavals, and wearing away of previous formations. It ended with long and widespread periods of erosion that made all of Arizona low and flat.

A sunset glows pink in the desert near Tucson.

Arizona Topography

Arizona is roughly divided into three major topographical zones: the basin and range, the central highlands, and the upper plateau regions. Each has its own unique features and beauty.

The southern third and western edge of the state are predominantly basin and range, characterized by parallel chains of mountain ranges interspersed with broad valleys and deserts that were created when portions of the earth's crust pulled away from each other. Set apart in a 70,000-square-mile "desert sea," the mountains of the basin and range have come to be known as "sky islands," globally unique mountain chains in southeastern Arizona, New Mexico, and Mexico. Because the mountains are isolated by vast expanses of deserts or grasslands, hundreds of flora and fauna are virtually trapped in the separate isolated environments of each range. Sky islands are the last North American stronghold for the Mexican wolf and the jaguar. Arizona's Chiricahua, Dragoon, Pinaleño, Santa Catalina, and Tumacacori ranges are home to more than forty sky islands.

The center of the state, particularly the eastern half, contains the mountainous central highlands. Caused by geologic uplifting, folding, and faulting, the highlands rest between 4,000 and 8,000 feet in elevation and receive more rain and snow than the rest of the state. Mountain ranges here are more tightly clustered than in the neighboring basin and range, with many valleys, canyons, lakes, and streams.

Northern Arizona is part of the vast Colorado Plateau, which spreads across the Four Corners states of Arizona, New Mexico, Colorado, and Utah. Ranging from 4,000 to 9,000 feet elevation, the Colorado Plateau is a land of far horizons and long vistas, where flat mesas and isolated rock spires rise from the red sandstone plateau, often capped with billowing banks of cumulous clouds. Monument Valley is the epitome of Colorado Plateau geology. The lightly populated plateau region is home to the Hopi and Navajo peoples, who bridge old and new, continuing their long-held traditions while at the same time engaging in innovative contemporary enterprises.

Because of its variety in terrain and elevation, Arizona hosts a diverse array of plants and animals. You can travel from low desert areas along the Colorado River at 70 feet above sea level to the treeless tundra of the San Francisco Peaks at 12,633 feet without leaving the state. Arizona's native species include 475 types of birds, 130 mammals, 90 reptiles, 80 fish, and 20 amphibians, along with thousands of plants.

Arizona is famous for its desert heat, celebrated each summer on the Route 66 town of Oatman's sidewalks with an egg-frying contest. Yet the state's higher elevations enjoy four distinct seasons, including autumn, when aspen-covered mountainsides turn golden, and pine-forested canyons are splashed with red maple. Even in the low desert, mountain ranges can be white-topped with winter

The Paleozoic Era (the Age of Fishes) followed the Precambrian, beginning about 500 million years ago. During this era oceans advanced and retreated as the continents tilted, overlapped, and finally formed one giant continent that geologists call Pangaea. The Grand Canyon's colorful upper cliffs and Sedona's red rocks are formed from Paleozoic strata.

Then came the Mesozoic Era (the Age of Reptiles), when dinosaurs roamed, leaving evidence in fossilized tracks and remains such as those discovered recently near the Arizona–Utah border. The Mesozoic was marked by turmoil, with monumental geologic uplift. Mountains and mesas were formed. Deserts alternated with swampy riversides. At the end of the Mesozoic, the tectonic plate under the North American continent broke away from Europe and collided with the Pacific Plate, creating more mountains and volcanoes.

Violent upheavals and uplifts continued in the Cenozoic Era (the Age of Mammals), which began 63 million years ago. Plateaus rose and basins dropped, while rivers and streams cut through uplifted rock to form dramatic chasms such as Grand Canyon and Canyon de Chelly.

snows. As early as February, spring creeps northward from the low deserts, heralded by colorful wildflowers such as fiery red Indian paintbrush and fields of golden poppies. The hot, dry foresummer in May and June is followed by the annual monsoon, when moisture moves up from the Gulf of California (Sea of Cortez) and the Gulf of Mexico, and dramatic afternoon thunderstorms sweep across the state until mid-September.

Ancient and Modern Indians

In 1908 an African-American ranch foreman named George McJunkin discovered large prehistoric bison bones in a stream in northeastern New Mexico, near the town of Folsom. Twenty years later, stone spearheads were found embedded in similar bones around the nearby town of Clovis. The spearheads belonged to nomadic Ice Age hunters, who roamed the Southwest at least 11,000 years ago. Anthropologists named them the Clovis Culture. In 1952 Dr. Emil Haury excavated a mammoth kill site near Naco, Arizona. He found Clovis Culture spear points among these ancient bones as well.

Navajo children often raise their own sheep to learn responsibility.

As the Southwest became warmer and drier, small semi-nomadic bands subsisted on smaller game and wild plants during the Archaic period, beginning sometime after 9000 B.C. Archaeological sites in Arizona and New Mexico have yielded a variety of projectile points and seed-processing tools.

Toward the end of the Archaic period, around 1000 B.C., people in the Southwest began farming. A more settled lifestyle eventually led them to construct year-round dwellings and make pottery, tools, and other items adapted to their local landscape and resources. Archaeologists classify and describe specific prehistoric cultures based on local and regional differences in pottery and other artifacts.

In what is now south-central Arizona, people known as the Hohokam (from an Akimel O'odham word meaning "those who have gone") built a network of irrigation canals for agriculture, as well as large public structures such as ballcourts and earthen platform mounds. Skilled Hohokam artisans created red-on-buff pottery, figurines, masks, and jewelry. Today's Akimel O'odham and Tohono O'odham people are believed to be descendants of the Hohokam.

The Ancestral Puebloans of northern Arizona (also referred to as the Anasazi) are known for their multistoried masonry dwellings, often built on top of hills or tucked inside cliff alcoves. They flourished in the Four Corners area until the 12th and early 13th centuries, when they abandoned their villages for reasons that archaeologists continue to debate, though drought is one likely factor.

The focus of Ancestral Puebloan culture shifted to New Mexico's Rio Grande Valley, Arizona's Hopi region, and the Zuni Mountains along the Arizona–New Mexico border, places where their Pueblo descendants live today. Spanish priests and colonists began arriving in the late 1500s, bringing significant European influence to Pueblo life.

Located between the Hohokam and Puebloan cultures, the Sinagua, Salado, and Mogollon cultures were influenced by their neighbors to the north and south. The Sinaguas lived in the area around the San Francisco Peaks and southward to the Verde Valley. The Sinagua villages flourished after A.D. 1150, leaving evidence of complex architecture and social organization. The Salado people occupied the Tonto Basin and Globe–Miami area, creating pueblos and cliff dwellings similar to those of their northern neighbors. The early Mogollons lived in pit houses, and later built pueblos in Arizona's central highlands and Little Colorado River valley, their region extending into Mexico and New Mexico.

By the early 1400s, Sinagua, Mogollon, and Salado villages were abandoned. Many villagers likely joined their Puebloan neighbors in the Hopi and Zuni regions, and some may have returned to a semi-nomadic lifestyle, hunting and gathering as their ancestors did, blending with other cultures entering the area.

The prehistoric Patayan people occupied the Colorado River Valley from Baja California to the Grand Canyon, practicing floodplain agriculture and traveling widely along the river corridor to hunt and trade. Though little is known about the Patayan culture, some archaeologists believe their descendants are the Yuman-speaking tribes of the Lower Colorado (Quechan, Mohave, and Cocopah) and the upland Pai (Havasupai and Hualapai) tribes.

Today over 300,000 Native Americans live in Arizona, many as part of the state's 22 federally recognized tribes, communities, and nations. Reservations and tribal communities make up more than a quarter of Arizona's lands throughout the state, though the amount of tribal land has been significantly reduced in some cases. The Navajo Nation, which spreads over the northeast corner of Arizona and into New Mexico and Utah, represents the largest tribe in the United States, with over 250,000 members.

Many tribes have retained aspects of their culture, including spiritual beliefs, traditions, clothing, livelihoods such as farming and ranching, and art forms such as world-renowned and highly prized weaving, pottery, basketry, and jewelry.

Above: San Xavier del Bac mission at dusk.

Opposite: Group portrait in front of the first passenger train to the Grand Canyon, September 1901.

Spanish Era: 1528-1821

In 1540 conquistador Francisco Vásquez de Coronado entered Arizona along the San Pedro River, searching for the fabled Seven Cities of Gold. His expedition, numbering over 1,000 men, failed to find the legendary cities. Through the expedition's reports, letters, and reconnaissance, however, Spain gained a foothold in the region.

Not all Spaniards traveled north in search of material riches. Jesuit and Franciscan missionaries sought converts, introducing the region's native peoples to Christianity. Missionaries found resistance among the Hopi people, who joined with the Rio Grande villages to throw out the Spanish in the Pueblo Revolt of 1680. But farther south, Father Francisco Eusebio Kino worked among the Akimel O'odham (also known as Pima) and Tohono O'odham (formerly known as Papago) peoples for nearly 25 years. In 1691 Father Kino established the mission of Tumacácori (now a national historic park) and in 1700, San Xavier del Bac, which still functions today as an active mission church. The missionaries introduced stock raising, new crops (including wheat and fruit trees), and Spanish culture.

But the Akimel O'odham and Tohono O'odham peoples rebelled in 1751, causing the Spanish to build a series of *presidios* (forts), the first in Tubac in 1752. Presidios protected a growing number of settlers, whose livestock had become a target for Apache raiders, who were now able to travel swiftly on Spanish horses.

The garrison relocated to Tucson in 1776 to extend Spain's northern frontier, and construction began on Presidio Real San Agustín del Tucsón. The presidio's eight- to twelve-foot-high adobe walls enclosed barracks for enlisted men, living space for officers and their families, and a chapel. Small farms and ranches outside the presidio's walls continued to lose livestock to raiders until Spanish leaders offered to trade rations for peace.

In 1810 unrest surged in New Spain, which included what is now Mexico, California, Nevada, Utah, and Arizona, and portions of present-day Wyoming, New Mexico, and Texas. *Mestizos* (people of combined European and Indian descent) and Indians living in New Spain revolted against Spain's treatment. Miguel Hidalgo, a Spanish priest, led the poor people in an uprising against the government. The Mexican War of Independence broke out with the assistance of New-World-born upper classes, and in 1821 the Republic of Mexico was born.

Mexican Era: 1821–1848

Bankrupted by years of war, the Mexicans could not afford to keep the peace with Apaches, so raiding and conflict resurged. The presidio of Tucson continued to protect a few hundred people, but southern Arizona mines and settlements were largely abandoned, and the Apaches and other tribes once again controlled the land.

Mexican independence also brought open commerce along the Santa Fe Trail. Mountain men from the expanding United States began exploring Mexico's northern frontier, following old Indian routes and blazing new trails in lands that included present-day Arizona, trapping animals for the fur trade. These trails were later used by the U.S. Army, gold and silver prospectors, and eventually settlers.

As a flood of immigrants sought a better life in America, editors and politicians urged them to "Go West," espousing the doctrine of Manifest Destiny—the belief that the United States was destined to expand across the North American continent. As a result of expansionist sentiments and actions, war between the United States and Mexico broke out in 1846. Colonel Stephen Watts Kearny was ordered to capture Nuevo México (which included present-day Arizona as well as New Mexico), and then proceed to Alta California. The war ended in 1848 with the Treaty of Guadalupe Hidalgo, ceding present-day California, Nevada, and Utah, plus parts of Wyoming, New Mexico, Arizona, and Texas to the United States. The Gadsden Purchase in 1854 extended Arizona's southern boundary from the Gila River to its present location.

American Era: 1848–present

After the Gadsden Purchase, Congress heard various proposals for dividing New Mexico Territory, which originally included Arizona. Growing animosity between northern and southern legislators complicated the debate. In 1861 secessionists in Tucson and Mesilla, New Mexico, declared the southern half of the territory for the Confederacy, and Tucson became the western capital of the Confederate Territory of Arizona.

As the Civil War raged in the East, the Union and Confederate armies battled for control of the West and its resources. Arizona offered a strategic overland route to California's gold fields. On April 15, 1862, a small picket of Rebels fought Union cavalry troops at Picacho Peak north of Tucson, the westernmost battle of the Civil War. Three Union soldiers were killed, and the Confederates returned to Tucson to warn the rest of the garrison. On learning 2,000 troops of the Union's First California Volunteers were approaching, the Confederates retreated to Texas.

In 1863 Congress divided New Mexico Territory along north-south lines, and Arizona became its own territory. The capital was moved north to Fort Whipple, far from Tucson's Confederate sympathizers and closer to the gold strikes made that year at the Hassayampa River, Lynx Creek, and other nearby streams near present-day Prescott and Wickenburg.

Following the war, more settlers arrived in Arizona Territory and staked claim to lands that Indian tribes had long used communally for hunting, gathering, and subsistence agriculture. Conflict raged, and according to military records thousands of U.S. troops flooded into Arizona. After a series of campaigns and skirmishes, most Indians surrendered and were confined to reservations, often a limited portion of their original homelands, where they were dependant on a system of inadequate government rations.

With new gold, silver, and copper discoveries, boomtowns sprang up all over the territory, from Oatman in northwestern Arizona to Bisbee in the southeast. Farming became big business as the influx of soldiers, prospectors, and shopkeepers needed food that they didn't have time to grow themselves. Ranchers sold their cattle to army forts, and the ranching business grew as the number of forts and soldiers increased. Railroads were built to serve the flood of goods and people.

In 1881 the Southern Pacific Railroad crossed the Arizona Territory. Before the railroad, people traveled by stagecoach, wagon train, or even steamboat on the Colorado River. The Southern Pacific and other railroads introduced Chinese laborers to Arizona, already a melting pot of Indians, Hispanics, Mormons, recent European immigrants, and other Anglos. Even rough boomtowns like Bisbee had opera houses and ladies' societies, but most Americans regarded Arizona Territory as a wild and dangerous place well into the early 1900s, still subject to bandits, shoot-outs, and merciless drought.

The taming of Arizona partly depended on providing supplemental water to farmers and ranchers. One of the first projects of the fledgling U.S. Bureau of Reclamation, Roosevelt Dam, allowed farming communities like Phoenix to expand and flourish. The Santa Fe Railway lured intrepid travelers with the promise of Western adventure and romanticized images of Indian cultures. Tourists and new residents were drawn by the mild climate, and health sanatoriums sprang up around Arizona, along with resorts and dude ranches. Eventually, Arizona would become known for its five Cs: copper, cattle, cotton, citrus, and climate.

As more people arrived and towns were built, the possibility of statehood beckoned. On February 14, 1912, Arizona at last became a state.

Arizona, "the Grand Canyon State," gets its nickname from its most spectacular wonder. Northwestern Arizona is home to the Grand Canyon and many other popular natural and manmade attractions. And yet the Grand Canyon region also holds the most remote land in the state. The Arizona Strip, as the stretch of land between the canyon and the Utah border is known, is physically cut off from the rest of the state. Two large manmade lakes flank the Grand Canyon on either side, where the Colorado River is held back first by Glen Canyon Dam and then by Hoover Dam. Though these lakes have greatly changed the river, they've added water recreation to a long list of area attractions.

Left and top: Agaves and collared lizards live in the canyon. Above: The Colorado River in Marble Canyon.

Grand Canyon

Many say the Grand Canyon is the planet's history book: 2 billion years are inscribed on the multicolored strata of its cliffs and canyons. One of the world's most visited natural wonders, this World Heritage Site holds an unmatched array of geological, historical, and biological treasures. Water, wind, plants, animals, and humans have all made their mark on the Grand Canyon in significant ways. All are part of this well-preserved history book, which also offers some of the most stunning visual spectacles on earth.

The Grand Canyon was formed by long sequences of weathering, erosion, sedimentation, volcanism, faulting, and uplifting. Eons of pushing up, wearing down, and washing away created the canyon we see today. The hardness and resistance of each type of rock determine what remains and what crumbles away. Geological forces continue to sculpt the Grand Canyon today. The river works at the bottom of the canyon, while weathering and erosion carve its walls.

The canyon's most powerful creative force, the Colorado River, winds 277 miles through Grand Canyon National Park, from Lees Ferry to Lake Mead. The river runs 1,450 miles from its source in the Rocky Mountains of Colorado to the Gulf of California, and drops over 13,000 feet in elevation over its course. In the Grand Canyon, its average width is 300 feet, and its average depth is 40 feet. The river became cleaner and more predictable after it was dammed upstream, but more than 160 heart-pumping white-water rapids still make the trip exciting. To preserve its beauty, the National Park Service limits the number of people who can boat through the canyon, but anyone who has run the rapids says it is worth the wait for a private permit or commercial trip to experience the thrill and wonder of floating through the Grand Canyon.

Above: The vivid turquoise water of Havasu Creek flows through Havasu Canyon before merging with the Colorado River in the Grand Canyon. Travertine, formed by calcium carbonate, coats the streambed, and the refraction of light gives the water its color.

Opposite: Agaves make their home on the cliffs above Marble Canyon.

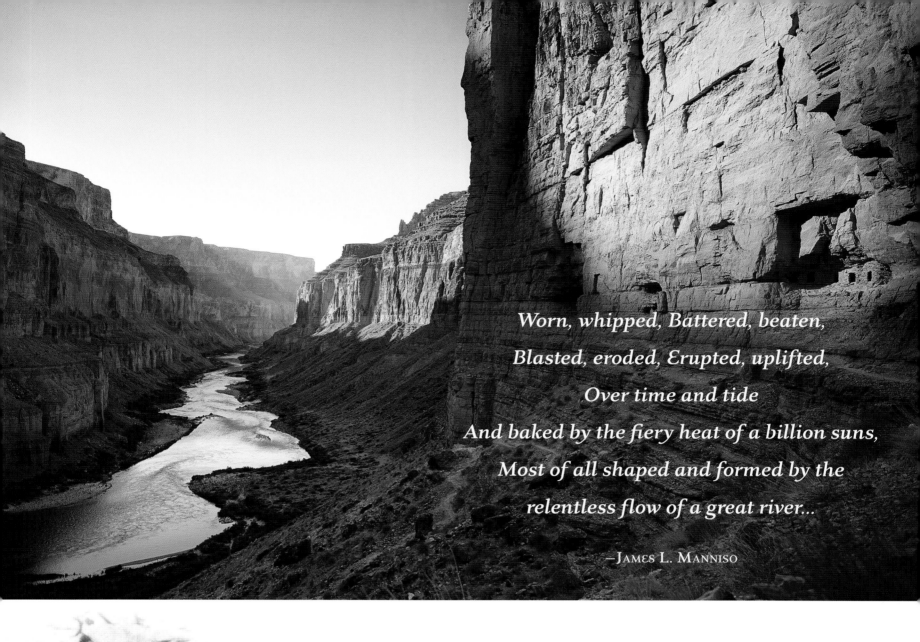

Worn, whipped, Battered, beaten,
Blasted, eroded, Erupted, uplifted,
Over time and tide
And baked by the fiery heat of a billion suns,
Most of all shaped and formed by the
relentless flow of a great river...

—JAMES L. MANNISO

The Grand Canyon's range of elevations, climates, and geological features allows a great biodiversity of plant and animal species to thrive. From desertscrub at the bottom of the canyon to spruce–fir forest on the North Rim, the canyon's biotic communities include 1,800 plant, 355 bird, 89 mammal, 47 reptile, 17 fish, and 19 amphibian species.

The Grand Canyon also has a lengthy human history. Four thousand years ago, Archaic hunters and gatherers wove small figures that looked like deer and mountain sheep out of split willow twigs. They pierced them with spear-like sticks, possibly as a ritual to ensure good hunting. These artifacts have been found in the recesses of the inner canyon.

Around A.D. 1, these same ancestors of the modern Pueblo and Hopi tribes began farming the Four Corners area (where Arizona, Utah, Colorado, and New Mexico meet), supplementing hunting and gathering with agriculture. They wove baskets and lived in caves or rock shelters. By approximately A.D. 500, they had added beans and cotton to their crops. They built circular pit houses, created clay pottery, and expanded their territory almost back to the Grand Canyon. With this more sedentary lifestyle, they produced ceramics and wove cotton cloth.

Ancestral Puebloans, named for their apartment-style villages, lived at the east end of the canyon around A.D. 700. By A.D. 1000, a large number of Ancestral Puebloans occupied hundreds of sites on both rims and in recesses in the canyon itself, moving seasonally from rim to river. The North Rim's Walhalla Glades and the South Rim's Tusayan Pueblo have provided archaeologists with clues about village life during this period. Puebloans and Cohoninas (a branch of the Patayan tradition) abandoned their villages around A.D. 1200, possibly because of drought.

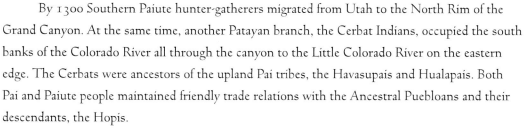

By 1300 Southern Paiute hunter-gatherers migrated from Utah to the North Rim of the Grand Canyon. At the same time, another Patayan branch, the Cerbat Indians, occupied the south banks of the Colorado River all through the canyon to the Little Colorado River on the eastern edge. The Cerbats were ancestors of the upland Pai tribes, the Havasupais and Hualapais. Both Pai and Paiute people maintained friendly trade relations with the Ancestral Puebloans and their descendants, the Hopis.

The canyon's historic period begins in 1540, when conquistador Francisco Vásquez de Coronado explored the West, claiming lands for King Charles V and searching for the fabled Seven Cities of Gold. Coronado sent Captain Garcia López de Cárdenas to the Grand Canyon's South Rim. Three of his soldiers hiked one-third of the way down before returning to report that a rock that looked as tall as a man from the rim was actually "bigger than the great tower of Seville." Though Europeans visited the Grand Canyon a few more times, they considered it little more than a travel obstruction.

In 1857 the U.S. Army sent Lieutenant Joseph Christmas Ives and a small crew up the Colorado River in a small paddle-wheeled steamboat. The expedition steamed up the Colorado to the rapids at Black Canyon (near where Hoover Dam is today), then continued on foot along the South Rim. In his report, Ives said, "Ours has been the first, and will doubtless be the last, party of whites to visit this profitless locality. It seems intended by nature that the Colorado River, along the greater part of its lonely and majestic way, shall be forever unvisited and undisturbed."

After the Civil War, Major John Wesley Powell, who had lost his right arm in battle, led the first known river trip through the Grand Canyon. On May 24, 1869, ten men in four boats started at Green River City, Wyoming, and followed the Green River until it merged with the Colorado River. In 1874 Powell's *Scribner's Monthly* articles about his canyon expeditions, illustrated with engravings drawn from Jack Hillers' photographs, brought national attention to the canyon's majestic beauty.

In 1886 Indiana senator (later U.S. president) Benjamin Harrison began the campaign to make the Grand Canyon a national park. Politics and private interests delayed the process, but President Harrison designated the area a forest reserve in 1893. In spite of this protection, damages occurred from permitted mining, grazing, and lumbering, as well as unchecked rim-side development.

To provide more protection for the canyon, President Theodore Roosevelt proclaimed the Grand Canyon a national monument in 1908 without the consent of Congress. For the next ten years various Grand Canyon National Park bills were fought out between private interests and the government. Finally, in 1919, Congress voted on a compromise, and President Woodrow Wilson signed the bill creating Grand Canyon National Park. During the Great Depression (1929–1941), the Civilian Conservation Corps built trails, picnic shelters, campgrounds, and telephone lines in the canyon, providing the park with valuable infrastructure. At the same time, commercial contractors built hotels and attractions.

The South & North Rims

Of the 5 million people who visit the Grand Canyon each year, most see it from the South Rim, the most easily accessible and developed part of the park. Crowds come here to gaze in awe on the great chasm. At an average elevation of 7,000 feet, the South Rim experiences the full range of seasons. Summer temperatures top out in the 80s (degrees F). July, August, and early September bring monsoonal thunderstorms, torrential rains, and flash floods. Winter temperatures dip into the teens but rise to the 40s (degrees F) due to sunny days. However, snow and ice are not uncommon, and the average annual snowfall is 50 to 100 inches or more, occasionally blanketing the canyon all the way down to the river below. The South Rim is home to pinyon–juniper woodland and ponderosa pine forest communities, with species such as gray fox, mule deer, bighorn sheep, and tassel-eared Abert squirrels.

The center of human activity on the South Rim is Grand Canyon Village. The Historic District was built by the Santa Fe Railway during the first half of the 20th century. The railroad partnered with the Fred Harvey Company to craft the canyon's image as a place of dramatic scenery and interesting cultures, providing tours and accommodations that highlighted Southwest themes.

The Harvey Company hired architect Mary Colter to design several buildings suited to the landscape. Colter's Lookout Studio, a gift shop and observation station, blends into the canyon's limestone rim. Railroad worker Bill Kent proposed to "Harvey Girl" waitress Betty Priest along the cliffs below Lookout Studio, but he always joked that *she* asked *him*, and threatened to push him over the edge if he didn't say yes!

Lookout Studio hugs the cliffs of the South Rim.

Above: View from Pima Point on the South Rim.

Below: Coyotes, commonly found in Arizona's deserts, also inhabit the Grand Canyon.

In 1901 Ellsworth Kolb arrived at the Grand Canyon and persuaded his brother Emery to join him the following year. They captured stunning photographs of the canyon and toured the East showing a movie of their boat trips through the canyon in the early 1900s. Emery Kolb showed the film several times a day for more than 60 years, making it the longest-running film in history. The brothers built Kolb Studio in stages to accommodate their growing business and Emery's family. It perches on the lip of the canyon next to Bright Angel Trail, where a small window allowed them to photograph the tourists who rode mules into the canyon.

Scenic Hermit Road winds along the rim for seven miles from Grand Canyon Village west to Hermits Rest. Private vehicles are allowed on this road only during winter months. During the rest of the year visitors may follow this route by free shuttle bus, foot, bicycle, or commercial tours. Hermits Rest offers a good view of Dripping Springs Canyon, where "the hermit," prospector Louis Boucher, lived around the turn of the 20th century. Mary Colter designed Hermits Rest in 1914 in the style of an old miner's cabin, incorporating an arch of uneven stones and a broken mission bell. When someone asked her, "Why don't you clean up this place?" she replied, "You can't imagine what it cost to make it look this old."

Desert View Drive is a scenic route that follows the rim for 25 miles east from Grand Canyon Village to the Desert View Watchtower. Private vehicles are permitted year-round. Mary Colter designed the watchtower, dedicated in 1933, as a replica of an Ancestral Puebloan tower. Colter flew over several prehistoric towers in a small plane before she visited them by car to sketch them and note building techniques. The 70-foot-tall watchtower blends in with the landscape while providing the widest possible view of the canyon. Artwork by Hopi painter Fred Kabotie graces the tower's first floor, and upper levels feature recreations of prehistoric pictographs.

The watchtower can be spotted from viewpoints along the higher and more remote North Rim. Though only ten miles across from the South Rim as the raven flies, it takes five hours to drive the 215 road miles from rim to rim. Hikers can also reach the North Rim by hiking 21 miles across the canyon from the South Rim. Only 10 percent of Grand Canyon visitors tour the North Rim, where they are rewarded by a quieter, off-the-beaten-path experience.

At an average elevation of 8,000 feet, the North Rim is higher and cooler than the South Rim. Summer temperatures top out in the 70s (degrees F), and winter highs stay closer to the freezing mark than at the South Rim. The North Rim is open to visitors only from mid-May through mid-October, when it is warmer and free of snow and ice.

The North Rim and the Kaibab Plateau host ponderosa pine forest, spruce–fir forest (blue spruce, Englemann spruce, Douglas fir, white fir, aspen, and mountain ash), mountain meadows (a rarity in Arizona), and grassland communities. Mountain lions, elk, and northern goshawks inhabit these communities. Kaibab squirrels, found only on the Kaibab Plateau, are cousins of the South Rim's Abert squirrels. As the inner canyon climate warmed up and dried out over the ages, the Kaibab subspecies evolved in geographic isolation.

Top: Aspen on the North Rim.

Above: Desert View Watchtower on the South Rim.

Below: Kaibab squirrels are unique to the North Rim and Kaibab Plateau.

Left: Pillars of Kaibab Limestone seen from Point Sublime on the North Rim.

The Inner Canyon

The more adventurous visitor can go beyond the sweeping vistas of the canyon's rims into its depths, exploring the inner canyon's rocks, waters, and caverns by foot, by mule, or by boat. The inner canyon plunges as much as 6,000 feet below the rim, exposing layers of geologic strata from the basement Vishnu Schist to the top layer of Kaibab Limestone. Phantom Ranch, a stopover point for hikers, mule riders, and river runners, sits nearly a mile below the rim. Architect Mary Colter designed this "deepest down ranch in the world" in 1922. It was built of local stone, but all other materials had to be brought down on mules.

Summer high temperatures at the river typically top 100 (degrees F). In winter, cold air gets trapped in the canyon, and high temperatures stay in the 40s and 50s, with lows in 30s and 40s. On rare occasions, snowfall makes it all the way down to the river.

The inner canyon is home to a variety of biotic communities. The river's edge hosts riparian vegetation and sandy beaches, with red-spotted toads, great blue herons, beavers, coyotes, and ringtails. Just above the river, Mojave and Great Basin desertscrub communities thrive, with a wide variety of cacti, desert shrubs, and trees, plus bats, rattlesnakes, lizards, and woodrats. Above the desertscrub, pinyon and juniper grow to elevations of 6,200 feet, and above that, ponderosa pine to 8,200 feet.

The three corridor trails—the North Kaibab, South Kaibab, and Bright Angel trails—all lead to Phantom Ranch at the bottom of the canyon; they are the only continuous trails that connect the North and South Rims, via two bridges that cross the Colorado. Mule trains make their way up and down the trails, carrying tourists, mail, or supplies. They travel almost a vertical mile from the river back to the trailhead at the rim.

Top: The Little Colorado River meets the Colorado River in the Grand Canyon.

Above and right: Blooming prickly pear cacti and red-spotted toads both call the inner canyon home.

Opposite: Royal Arch Creek in Elves Chasm.

Above: Travertine terraces below Havasu Falls in Havasu Canyon.

Right: First light on a wickiup at Eagle Point on the Hualapai Reservation.

Opposite: The ringtail, Arizona's state mammal, inhabits the inner reaches of Grand and Havasu canyons. Havasu Falls' flow and appearance change with the seasons and with each summer flood.

Havasu Canyon & Grand Canyon West

Outside park boundaries on the western end of the canyon, the Havasupai and Hualapai Indian Reservations offer unique attractions. Often referred to as a Shangri-la, or paradise, Havasu Canyon is a large tributary on the south side of the Colorado River, located within the Havasupai Indian Reservation. It can be accessed only by foot, mule, horse, or helicopter. Havasupai means "people of the blue-green waters," referring to the vivid turquoise water of Havasu Creek. Travertine, formed by calcium carbonate, coats the streambed, and the refraction of light gives the water its color. Tribal members and their ancestors have lived in the canyon and on the rim for several hundred years. The Havasupais spent summers at the bottom of Havasu Canyon and winters up on the plateau until 1882, when they were confined to the canyon on a tiny reservation. In 1975 some of their plateau lands were finally returned to them. Today, tourism is a major source of revenue to the Havasupais, as each year thousands visit the village of Supai to explore the nearby idyllic pools and waterfalls.

Further west along the rim, the large Hualapai ("people of the tall pine") reservation extends down to the Colorado River. The Hualapais are related linguistically to the Havasupai and Yavapai peoples, all part of the Yuman language family. The Colorado River is significant to the Hualapais as the location of their creation story. Historically, the Hualapais hunted and gathered on the plateau in winter, and farmed in the canyon in summer. Today their economy is based on cattle ranching, timber, arts and crafts, and tourism at Grand Canyon West, an area developed to take in the views from Quartermaster Point. The highlight is the Grand Canyon Skywalk, a horseshoe-shaped cantilevered glass bridge jutting 70 feet out from the rim. Completed in 2007, it can support up to 71 million pounds, and the two-inch-thick steel frame is topped with 46 panes of five-layered laminated glass to provide a crystal-clear view of the canyon floor 3,600 feet below. The Skywalk is located 121 miles east of Las Vegas, Nevada, and 242 miles west of the South Rim Visitor Center.

Glen Canyon & Lake Powell

On his first voyage down the Colorado River, John Wesley Powell noted this area's "carved walls, royal arches, glens, alcove gulches, mounts and monuments" and named it Glen Canyon. Though many of the beautiful rock formations of Glen Canyon that so impressed Powell are now submerged, the lake that bears his name has become one of the most popular recreational sites in the Southwest. Lake Powell was formed after Glen Canyon Dam was built on the Colorado River in the 1950s to supply water and electricity to Arizona's cities. Houseboaters, water-skiers, and jet-skiers frequent the lake, which has five marinas near Page, Arizona, and in bordering Utah. Lake Powell is the continent's second-largest manmade lake, at 186 miles long, with more than 1,000 miles of shoreline.

Several unique rock features still rise above the waters of Lake Powell, including Tower Butte and Gunsight Butte. Rainbow Bridge National Monument (just across the Utah border), is the world's largest rock arch at 290 feet high. The sandstone bridge is sacred to the Navajos, who call it Nonnezoshi, which means "rainbow turned to stone."

Glen Canyon Dam transformed the warm, sediment-laden, flood-prone Colorado into a cool, clear, relatively tame river below the dam. This change impacted the flora and fauna in and around the river, and also the beaches along the river, which erode more severely without the replenishment of the sediment now trapped behind the dam. On the other hand, predictable flows have made commercial raft trips through the Grand Canyon possible, and aquatic and migratory birds that were previously absent from Glen Canyon are now drawn to the waters of Lake Powell. For 15 miles below the dam, a stretch of flat water passes through the remaining unflooded section of Glen Canyon, giving boaters a sense of what John Wesley Powell experienced on his 1869 voyage.

Dominated by the rosy-tan Navajo sandstone that forms the canyon's sheer cliffs and sculpted buttes, Glen Canyon's rock layers preserve fossils from the Mesozoic Era (248 to 65 million years ago). Spring-fed hanging gardens grow out of vertical cliff walls streaked with tapestries of desert varnish (a patina of dark iron and manganese oxides). These gardens support at least ten species unique to the Glen Canyon area, and walls bear petroglyphs made by ancient cultures.

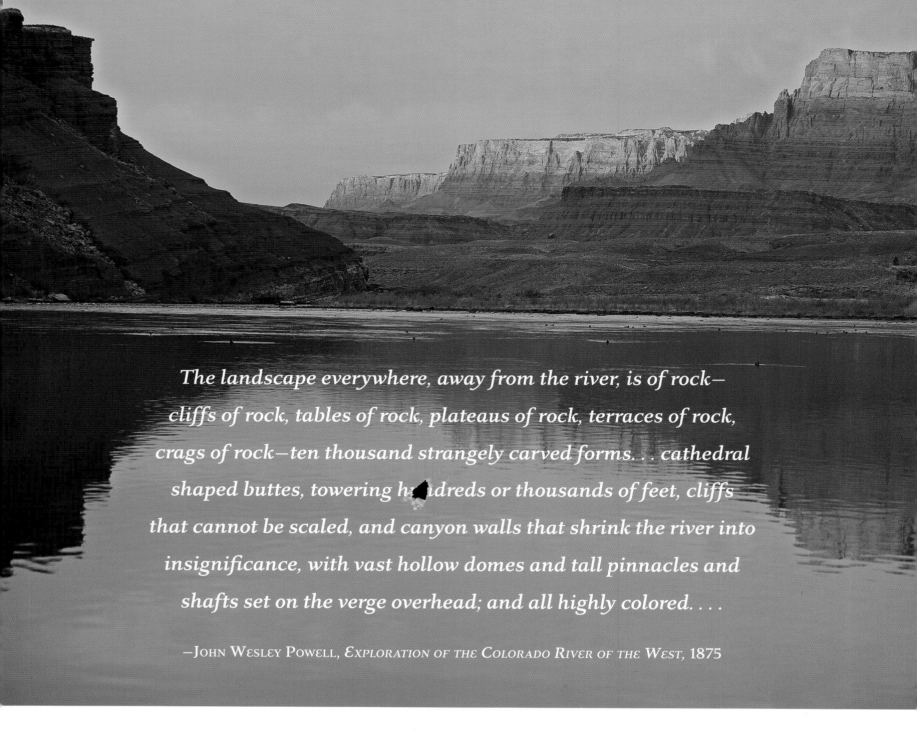

The landscape everywhere, away from the river, is of rock—
cliffs of rock, tables of rock, plateaus of rock, terraces of rock,
crags of rock—ten thousand strangely carved forms. . . cathedral
shaped buttes, towering hundreds or thousands of feet, cliffs
that cannot be scaled, and canyon walls that shrink the river into
insignificance, with vast hollow domes and tall pinnacles and
shafts set on the verge overhead; and all highly colored. . . .

—JOHN WESLEY POWELL, *EXPLORATION OF THE COLORADO RIVER OF THE WEST*, 1875

Lees Ferry with the Vermilion Cliffs beyond.

Marking the western end of Glen Canyon is Lees Ferry, a historical Colorado River crossing. Mormon trailblazer Jacob Hamblin crossed here in 1864. His route later became known as the Honeymoon Trail, used by Mormon families traveling to and from new settlements in Arizona. In 1871 John Doyle Lee arrived at the crossing, hiding from federal authorities after being implicated in the Mountain Meadows Massacre, in which a group of Mormons and Paiute allies murdered a party of non-Mormon emigrants from Missouri. Lee claimed, as many others suspected, that he was merely a scapegoat. Lee operated a ferry across the river until he was apprehended in 1874 and later executed. Lee's fourth wife, Emma, continued operating the ferry, which was used until it sank in 1928. For several months, travelers had to detour 800 miles to reach the other side of the Colorado. Then, on January 12, 1929, Navajo Bridge was completed over the river across Marble Canyon, linking the isolated Arizona Strip to the rest of the state.

Today, the National Park Service manages Lees Ferry as a historical site within the Glen Canyon National Recreation Area, offering a campground, boat launch, and several hiking trails. One trail leads to the remains of Lonely Dell, John and Emma Lee's ranch. Lees Ferry is the principal starting point for whitewater rafting trips through the Grand Canyon, as well as one of the few places in the canyonlands where you can drive to a beach and watch the great Colorado River flow by.

Above: A hiker along the Paria River, deep in Paria Canyon.

Below: The rock of Coyote Buttes seems to swirl like water in Paria Canyon.

Vermilion Cliffs

The aptly named Vermilion Cliffs rise high above Lees Ferry. Administered by the Bureau of Land Management, Vermilion Cliffs National Monument encompasses nearly 300,000 acres of magnificent sandstone foundations, canyons, and cliffs ranging from 3,000 to 6,500 feet in elevation. The monument is situated along the Colorado and Paria rivers, northeast of the Grand Canyon between Page, Arizona, and Kanab, Utah. Spelled "Pahreah" on older documents and pronounced like Maria, Paria means "muddy water" in the Paiute language. The sediment-laden Paria joins the Colorado at Lees Ferry in a swirling confluence of light brown and blue-green waters.

The monument is home to bighorn sheep, pronghorn antelope, and 20 varieties of raptors. Endangered California condors were reintroduced here in 1994, and the cliffs make a beautiful backdrop for viewing the huge black birds. The Vermilion Cliffs get their intense colors from iron oxide, manganese, and other minerals, forming one of the "steps" in the Grand Staircase, a series of sedimentary rock layers that stretch from Utah's Bryce Canyon National Park to the Grand Canyon.

Located mostly within monument boundaries, the Paria Canyon–Vermilion Cliffs Wilderness is a favorite destination of backpackers because of its deep, narrow canyons, red sand beaches, and fantastic purple, red, and black cliffs.

Lake Mead

On the opposite end of the Grand Canyon, Hoover Dam holds back the Colorado River to create Lake Mead, the continent's largest manmade lake. The dam, named after President Herbert Hoover, was built to supply water and electricity to the Southwest. When the dam was completed in 1936, it was the world's largest concrete structure, at 764 feet high and 1,244 feet wide at the top.

Lake Mead National Recreation Area extends west from the Grand Wash Cliffs, which mark the end of the Grand Canyon, to hug the Arizona–Nevada border along 140 miles of the Colorado River's original course. Lake Mead's waters appear jewel-blue against the stark Mojave Desert setting of deep canyons, dry washes, rugged cliffs, distant mountain ranges, colorful soils, and rock formations. Animals living in the Mojave Desert, such as desert bighorn sheep and collared lizards, have adapted to tolerate heat and conserve water. Though less than six inches of rain falls each year, spring wildflowers add dashes of red, yellow, and lavender to a landscape dominated by cacti, creosote, and Joshua trees.

When full, Lake Mead is 110 miles long, with 550 miles of shoreline marked by beaches and coves that invite boaters to linger. Smaller and narrower Lake Mohave, at 67 miles long, was created by Davis Dam and is also part of the recreation area. Lake Mohave seems more river than lake, retaining some of the Colorado's original characteristics. Kayakers and hikers enjoy exploring the springs and seeps of striking Black Canyon, which begins at the lake's upper reaches, in the shadow of Hoover Dam. ✳

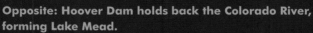

Opposite: Hoover Dam holds back the Colorado River, forming Lake Mead.

Above: A kayaker floats through Emerald Cave on the Colorado River in Black Canyon, near Lake Mead.

Left: Brightly colored collared lizards live in the hot deserts of Arizona.

High Country

Just a few hours' drive south of the Grand Canyon, a swath of green mountains stretches across the center of Arizona, marking the transition zone between the Colorado Plateau and basin and range country. Vast stands of ponderosa pine thrive along the plateau's rocky edge, known as the Mogollon Rim, from the high forests of Flagstaff to the lush White Mountains. Below the rim are the red rocks of Sedona, and further south, the Verde Valley and the mining towns of Prescott and Jerome.

Left: Sedona's Cathedral Rock. Top: Alligator juniper berries. Above: San Francisco Peaks.

People have lived in these mountains since prehistoric times. Ancient cultures occupied and then abandoned high country villages repeatedly for centuries, then bands of Yavapais and Apaches roamed the same canyons and valleys. Anglos answered the call of gold there, settling in towns and on ranches. Following the California Gold Rush, gold strikes in northern Arizona attracted prospectors hoping to get rich overnight. At the northern edge of basin and range country, the Bradshaw Mountains, the Sierra Prietas, and the Black Hill range yielded some of Arizona's greatest mineral discoveries.

In 1926 as roads were being built all over the country to accommodate the growing number of automobiles, Route 66 was completed, linking Chicago with Los Angeles. In northern Arizona, Route 66 passed through deserts, forests, and plateaus, following the old Beale Wagon Road, an army route that once led from Fort Defiance westward to the Colorado River. Route 66 paved the way to a fresh start in California and became a popular route for travelers hoping to "get your kicks," as the Bobby Troup song proclaims. In the 1950s, however, the construction of Interstate 40 drove Route 66 into legend. Some of the longest and best-preserved sections of the so-called Mother Road travel through Arizona near Williams, Ash Fork, Seligman, Kingman, and other charming towns that serve up a slice of history, along with a malted milk or cup of joe at classic diners designed with plenty of chrome and flashy jukeboxes.

Today Arizona's mountain country draws droves of visitors each year from around the world. Hikers, anglers, art lovers, New Age spiritualists, and history buffs looking for a taste of the West can all find something here to enjoy and appreciate.

Top: The Wigwam Hotel on historic Route 66.
Above: Palatki Ruin, a Sinagua cliff dwelling near Sedona.
Opposite: Oak Creek bursts with color in autumn.

Sedona

Sedona is a tourist mecca, art town, and resort community nestled among fantastic red rock formations. The steep, winding road from Flagstaff to Sedona through Oak Creek Canyon drops 2,000 feet from pine forests to desert vegetation in 30 miles, threading between fault-formed cliffs and the dappled shadows of oaks, cottonwoods, and sycamores. Sedona's famed red sandstone buttes and spires are carved from the southern edge of the Colorado Plateau and bear such colorful names as Coffee Pot, Bell Rock, and Snoopy. (It takes very little imagination to see him lying on his back on top of his doghouse.)

At 4,000 to 6,000 feet in elevation, Sedona experiences a moderate climate with four seasons. Its range of elevation and terrain support a variety of plant communities, including desert grassland, oak woodland, and ponderosa pine and spruce–fir forests. Pinyon–juniper woodland predominates, home to ravens, quail, javelinas, coyotes, and deer. Spring-fed Oak Creek flows south through Oak Creek Canyon before joining the Verde River near Cottonwood. The creek's riparian community includes trout, great blue herons, and ringtail cats (part of the raccoon

Left: View of Sedona's famous red rocks from Thunder Mountain.

Opposite left and below: Oak Creek is home to a vital riparian community.

family). The Sedona area is home to 500 plant, 55 mammalian, 180 bird, 35 reptile and amphibian, 20 fish, and thousands of native insect and invertebrate species.

Because of the Sedona area's rich resources, ancient peoples here long relied on wild foods such as agave, yucca, nuts, and berries before slowly making the transition to agriculture. Ancient paleo and archaic peoples used caves and rock overhangs as shelters, leaving little evidence of their time in the Sedona area. Palatki, a cultural site under the protection of Coconino National Forest, is a southern Sinagua cliff dwelling with associated pictographs and petroglyphs. Around A.D. 1300, the Sinaguas relocated to large hilltop villages near creeks and rivers, and Yavapais and Tonto Apaches moved into the Verde Valley. Small bands of Yavapais and Tonto Apaches roamed widely across hills and valleys in search of game and seasonal plants.

The traditional lifestyle of the Yavapais and Apaches contrasted sharply—and at times violently—with that of Anglo homesteaders. The army established forts to protect settlements associated with nearby mines. General George Crook, nicknamed "Gray Fox" by the Apaches, commanded Fort Verde from 1871 to 1873, using Indian scouts to locate rival bands and tribes. Many Yavapais and Tonto Apaches were forced onto the Rio Verde Reservation. Further south, dozens of Yavapais were killed by the U.S. Army in the brutal Skeleton Cave Massacre. On February 27, 1875, the army compelled the Yavapais and Tonto Apaches to begin a 150-mile journey from the Rio Verde Reservation to the San Carlos Apache Reservation, marching them through icy, flooding streams and rugged mountains. Many died during the two-week trek and 25 babies were born along what the Yavapai and Apache people call their Exodus. At San Carlos, poor land and pestilential water created famine and epidemics. Eventually, around the turn of the 20th century, some Yavapais were able to return to Prescott, the Verde Valley, and the Fort McDowell area north of Phoenix. By this time, the farming community of Sedona and the mining town of Jerome were already established, and the Indians' traditional lifeways existed only in story.

Below: General George Crook.

There must be places for human beings
to satisfy their souls.

—JOHN MUIR

After the army moved the Indians out, more Anglos moved in. When Jim Thompson settled in Oak Creek Canyon in 1876, he found an abandoned plot of vegetables still growing. He named his small farm Indian Gardens. In 1884 Henry Schuerman acquired a farm farther downstream, an area that became known as Red Rock. Other families settled between Red Rock and Oak Creek Canyon. At the turn of the century, the Schnebly family moved into the area, building one of the earliest frame homes, from which they offered rooms to travelers and sold a few groceries. T. C. Schnebly, the first postmaster, named the growing community after his wife, Sedona.

Sedona's beautiful red rocks began attracting artists, filmmakers, and wealthy people seeking vacation retreats. The Chapel of the Holy Cross, constructed in 1956, was conceived by sculptor Marguerite Brunswick Staude, a student of architect Frank Lloyd Wright. The circular walkway to the chapel and the great window behind the altar offer panoramic views. In 1978 the Spanish colonial-style art village of Tlaquepaque was completed. Tlaquepaque's sycamore-shaded courtyards and bubbling fountains provide a soothing setting for art galleries, shops, and restaurants.

In the 1970s Sedona's reputation as a center for spiritual growth and alternative healing methods grew along with the New Age movement. Many people travel to Sedona to visit "vortex sites" (places reputed to hold heightened earth energy), participate in a meditation or yoga retreat, or experience bodywork therapies at a spa or resort. Considering the beauty of Sedona's natural setting, it isn't surprising that many attribute healing powers to its red rocks. As conservationist John Muir once said, "There must be places for human beings to satisfy their souls."

Whether soul-searching or adventuring, visitors to Sedona will find a 500-square-mile scenic wonderland with acres of national forest, designated wilderness, and state parks, offering a range of activities from hiking and camping to scenic drives. Slide Rock State Park is a popular family destination, where the creek tumbles gently over polished-smooth rocks, making a natural water slide.

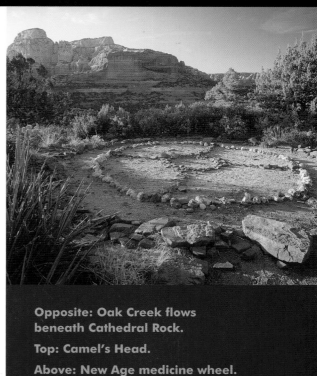

Opposite: Oak Creek flows beneath Cathedral Rock.
Top: Camel's Head.
Above: New Age medicine wheel.

Verde Valley & Prescott

Across the Verde Valley from Sedona, the former copper-mining town of Jerome perches on the side of Mingus Mountain. Though conquistador Antonio Espejo reported rich copper deposits here in 1583, the mining camp of Jerome wasn't established until 1883. The need for copper wire for telephones and electric lights caused a worldwide mining boom, and by the late 1920s, Jerome was the fourth-largest city in Arizona. By the time the mines closed in the early 1950s, Jerome had become one of the richest mining areas in the world, producing more than $1 billion in copper, gold, and silver. Ten years later, "the wickedest town in the West" was nearly a ghost town, but hippies and artists moved into the abandoned buildings and kept it alive. Those members of the so-called counterculture became Jerome's leading citizens, sparking historic preservation and revitalization efforts. Today, Jerome has been reborn as an art community and tourist destination.

Below Mingus Mountain are the Verde Valley communities of Clarkdale, Cottonwood, and Camp Verde, linked by the Verde River, which runs 283 miles south to reservoirs near Cave Creek, outside of Phoenix. Whatever water escapes the Cave Butte Dam meets the Salt River, then the Gila, in a weak attempt to reach the confluence with the Colorado River. Along its route, the Verde River (designated a Wild and Scenic River by Congress in 1984) provides a riparian habitat with cottonwoods and willows, attracting wildlife such as bald eagles, black hawks, and other threatened or endangered species. Running north along the river from Clarkdale, the recreational Verde

View from Jerome, with Sedona's red rocks visible in the distance.

Canyon Railroad offers glimpses of wildlife and history. Every April, Cottonwood hosts a birding festival, with field trips and workshops that center on the Verde Valley's ecological riches.

High above a bend in the Verde River lie the remains of a sprawling hilltop village known as Tuzigoot (Apache for "crooked water"). The Sinagua people began to build this village, now a national monument, around A.D. 1000, using the river's water to irrigate their crops. A few miles to the southeast, near Camp Verde, the Sinaguas built Montezuma Castle high in the limestone cliffs above Beaver Creek. This striking four-story, multiroom dwelling was once a popular sightseeing locale for soldiers and families stationed at Fort Verde, who likely named it after the Aztec ruler Montezuma. Both villages were abandoned in the 1400s, for unclear reasons that continue to intrigue archaeologists. Montezuma Castle National Monument is one of Arizona's most popular treasures.

A few miles to the northeast along Beaver Creek, a separate unit of the monument protects Montezuma Well. The well is a sinkhole, a collapsed underground limestone cavern filled with water, measuring 368 feet across and 55 feet deep. Dissolved carbon dioxide levels 600 times higher than most aquatic environments preclude many aquatic animals, especially fish, from living in these waters. Instead, the well supports a unique ecosystem with plants and animals found nowhere else on earth. A wide variety of leeches, amphipods (brine shrimp), water scorpions, and turtles live in this enclosed ecosystem.

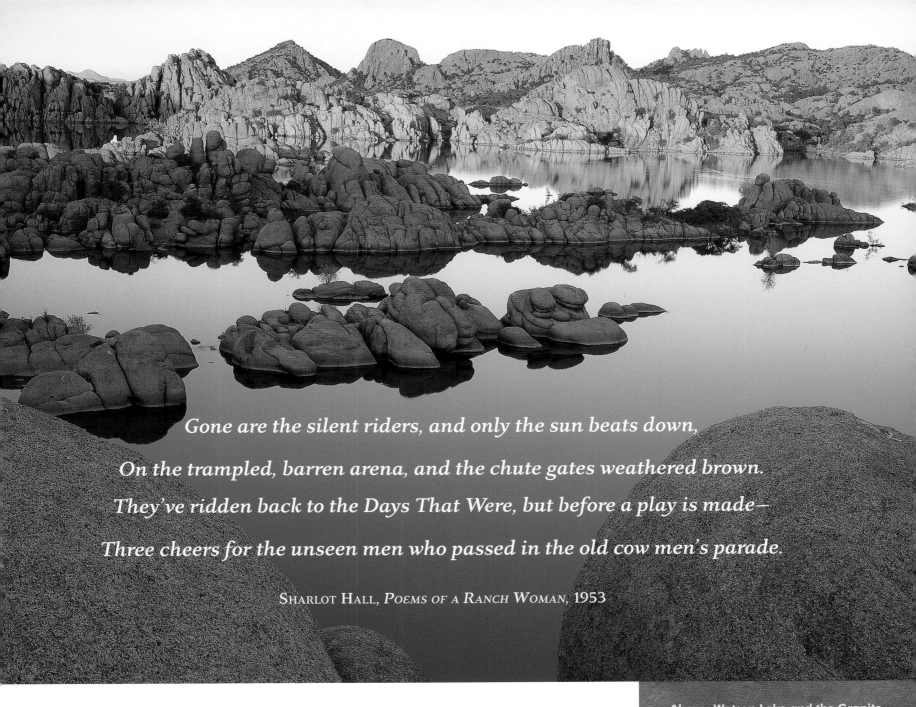

Gone are the silent riders, and only the sun beats down,

On the trampled, barren arena, and the chute gates weathered brown.

They've ridden back to the Days That Were, but before a play is made—

Three cheers for the unseen men who passed in the old cow men's parade.

SHARLOT HALL, *POEMS OF A RANCH WOMAN*, 1953

Above: Watson Lake and the Granite Dells in Prescott. Below: Yavapai County courthouse, with statue of Bucky O'Neil (a Rough Rider in the Spanish–American War).

From A.D. 900 to 1400, a community of more than 200 Sinaguas lived at Montezuma Well. Visitors can take a half-mile loop trail to the water's edge and examine well-preserved prehistoric rooms built in caves or under rock ledges. Other dwellings perch just below the rim of the well's 200-foot walls. The well figures prominently in creation stories handed down by generations of Yavapai and Apache people, and may be the ancestral home of clans residing on the Hopi Mesas.

West of Verde Valley, Prescott played an important role in Arizona's more recent history. In 1863 the army established Fort Whipple to protect miners from Yavapai and Apache attacks, and months later nearby Prescott became the territorial capital, close to nearby gold discoveries and far from Tucson's hotbed of Confederate sympathizers. The governor's mansion—a large log cabin—is preserved at the Sharlot Hall Museum, along with a schoolhouse, printing press, and other vestiges of territorial life. A short walk leads to Whiskey Row, once a red-light district of 40 saloons immortalized in verse by cowboy poet Gail Gardner: "Oh, they starts her in at the Kaintucky bar at the head of Whiskey Row, and they winds up down by the Depot House some forty drinks below." Across the street, the stately county courthouse lawn is the scene of several summertime festivals. Each July, Prescott hosts one of the world's oldest rodeos, held since 1888.

Flagstaff & the
San Francisco Peaks

The arrival of the Santa Fe Railway in 1881 put Flagstaff on the map. Situated near the largest stand of ponderosa pine in the world, Flagstaff needed the railroad to transport its major products, timber and cattle, to market. Within five years, Flagstaff was the largest town on the main line between Albuquerque and the Pacific. In 1896 Flagstaff's history as a science center began when Boston millionaire Percival Lowell built an observatory on Mars Hill to observe space through the dry, dark, clear skies. Pluto was discovered here in 1930. Northern Arizona University, founded in 1899, drew foresters and geologists.

Anthropologists and archaeologists arrived in the early 20th century to excavate prehistoric ruins, carting so many artifacts back East that the Museum of Northern Arizona was established in 1928 with a mission of preserving and protecting regional cultural sites.

Today, Flagstaff is a college town and a playground for outdoor enthusiasts, including skiers, river runners, and mountain bikers. It is also a major stopover on the transcontinental Interstate 40, which replaced the old Route 66 in this area.

Dominating the skyline north of Flagstaff, the San Francisco Peaks are the centerpiece of an 1,800-square-mile volcanic field with some 600 cinder cones, as well as lava domes, ice caves, and other volcanic features. The San Franciscos' four-peak cluster was once one huge symmetrical stratovolcano similar to Japan's Mount Fujiyama. Spanish friars living at the Hopi Mesas in 1629 named the peaks Sierra Sin Agua de San Francisco, the "mountains without water," honoring the patron saint of the Franciscan order. Humphreys Peak, at an elevation of 12,633 feet, is the highest point in Arizona. At 11,400 feet, the tree line ends and tundra begins, and it may snow here any day of the year. Hopis regard the peaks as the home of the Kachina spirits, and Navajos consider them their sacred mountain of the west.

Top left: Aspens grow on the mountains' slopes.

Middle left: Ponderosa pine trees in front of Ashurst Lake, with the San Francisco Peaks in the distance.

Bottom left: Greater short-horned lizard in Flagstaff's ponderosa pine forest.

Above: Snow can fall any time of the year on the highest reaches of the San Francisco Peaks.

The volcanic field's most recent cinder cone is Sunset Crater, a prime example of Arizona's dramatic geology. Recent evidence indicates that the Sunset Crater volcano erupted between A.D. 1080 and 1150, forming a cone more than 1,000 feet high. The volcano spewed out a blanket of ash and debris that covered 800 square miles and forced the Sinaguas to abandon many of their settlements for several years.

Adjoining Sunset Crater National Monument is Wupatki National Monument. Here, on a remote volcanic plain in the north, stands the impressive ancient ruin called Wupatki (Hopi for "big house"). This many-roomed structure is made of precisely fitted slabs of red sandstone. Archaeologists estimate that more than 2,000 people, a mixture of Ancestral Puebloan, Sinagua, and Cohonina, immigrated here after the Sunset Crater volcano erupted. Wupatki was located along an ancient trade route with links to villages throughout the Southwest. Artifacts indicate that these ancient peoples traded pottery, beads, and turquoise for copper bells and parrots from Mexico and abalone shells from the California coast. The Wupatki ballcourt is the northernmost example of its kind, similar to those found in Mexico and Central America.

East of Flagstaff another impressive crater marks the high desert landscape. Meteor Crater—4,000 feet in diameter and 570 feet deep—was originally thought to be the result of volcanic action. Then, in the 1890s, Daniel M. Barringer suggested that an iron-bearing meteorite created the huge depression. His theory was finally proven by Eugene M. Shoemaker in 1960 with the discovery of rare forms of quartz formed by high impact.

Also in the 1960s, lunar-mission astronauts trained in the crater, and scenes for the 1984 movie *Star Man* were filmed here. Meteor Crater was an attraction on the Fred Harvey Company's famed Indian Detours, which were launched from nearby Winslow in the 1930s. Guests rode in specially outfitted Harveycars and stayed at La Posada, architect Mary Colter's favorite hotel, now lovingly restored.

Above: Sunset Crater.
Right: Box Canyon ruins during a summer storm at Wupatki National Monument.

Above: **Fishing on Big Lake.**

Below: **Locoweed flowers.**

Right: **Golden eagles and mountain lions are two of the White Mountains' predators.**

The White Mountains

At the east end of the Mogollon Rim, the White Mountains, Arizona's largest range, span approximately 120 miles east to west and 40 miles north to south in some places. The White Mountains are more humpbacked ridges than sharp peaks, covered with forests of ponderosa pine and quaking aspens, and interspersed with grassy meadows where deer, pronghorn, and elk make their home. The streams, springs, and wetlands host a diverse array of plant and animal species, such as the Apache trout (Arizona's state fish) and the rare Chiricahua leopard frog. Sadly, the last grizzly bear in Arizona was killed in the White Mountains in the 1930s. Mexican gray wolves, which had also been eliminated from the area, are now being reintroduced.

Many important rivers are born in the White Mountains. The Little Colorado River flows northwest from a spring at Mount Baldy (11,590 feet), to join the main Colorado River in the Grand Canyon. The Black River meets the White River in Apacheland, and flows southwest to form the Salt River. The Blue River flows south from Sierra Azul ("blue range"), on the east side of the White Mountains, to converge with the Gila River.

In 1870 in an effort to secure U.S. interests against attacks by Apaches and other tribes, the U.S. military began construction of a camp in the White Mountains, strategically placed

between Navajo country in the north and Apache tribes in the south. On his first visit to the camp in 1871, General Crook enlisted Apache men to serve as scouts, a tactic that would help the U.S. Army win the Apache Wars. The post was officially designated Fort Apache in 1879. After it was decommissioned in 1922, the Apache scouts transferred to Fort Huachuca in southern Arizona, where they served until 1947. Today, the White Mountain Apache Reservation covers more than two-thirds of these mountains. The summit of Mount Baldy is sacred to Apaches, and only tribal members are allowed to climb to the top.

The White Mountains have been a destination for generations of Arizonans, who ski the slopes of the tribally owned Sunrise Ski Resort and make summer retreats to cabins or lodges in Greer, Alpine, and other nearby towns. Excellent fishing in the numerous lakes and streams attracts anglers, while hiking, mountain biking, horseback riding, camping, skiing, and sightseeing make the White Mountains Arizona's ideal recreation haven.

Wind, sand, dust, gravel, pebbles

—watch out for your eyes!

—ZANE GREY, *THE HERITAGE OF THE DESERT*, 1910

Mogollon Rim

The Mogollon Rim is the 7,000-foot-high edge of the Colorado Plateau, an escarpment that slashes diagonally across central Arizona from Sedona to the White Mountains. The rim is defined by straight buff-colored cliffs of Coconino Sandstone and Kaibab Limestone. Nearly 200 miles long and cut by rugged canyons, the rim borders the scrub and pine belt of the Arizona Transition Zone. Overlooking the Tonto Basin, 2,000 to 3,000 feet below, and the deserts beyond, the rim boasts some of the state's most far-reaching views. Several fine overlooks lie along the mostly unpaved Rim Road, which edges the cliffs and parallels sections of the historic General Crook Trail.

Rim Country was popularized by Western author Zane Grey, who once owned a cabin near Christopher Creek. An avid outdoorsman, Grey's adventures inspired his best-selling novels and popular magazine articles. One of his 64 novels, *To the Last Man* (1921), was loosely based on the Pleasant Valley range war that occurred between herders, ranchers, and cattle rustlers in the Tonto Basin.

The rim's friendly small towns welcome desert dwellers seeking relief from the summer heat. Sitting just below the rim, Payson is a gateway to its creeks, reservoirs, and forests, as well as a jumping-off point for hiking and backpacking trips into the Matzatzal Mountains. ❋

Above right: Writer Zane Grey.

Above: Aspens at sunrise, Blue Vista on the Mogollon Rim.

Right: Abert squirrels, cousins of the Kaibab Plateau's Kaibab squirrel, inhabit the forests of Arizona's high country.

Indian Country

High on the Colorado Plateau, the Navajo and Hopi reservations stretch across Arizona's northeastern corner. The plateau hosts a wide variety of vegetation, from desert grassland to conifer forests. Wild plants, once essential for food, medicine, and fuel, continue to play an integral role in cultural practices. Pinyon-juniper woodlands are widespread in Indian Country. People of the plateau continue to harvest pinyon nuts in the fall, an activity thousands of years old. Yucca, another common plateau plant, is still collected by the Navajos and Hopis for such purposes as basketry, paintbrushes for pottery decoration, and as part of a Navajo girl's coming-of-age ceremony.

Top: Datura flower. Above: Navajo sandstone. Right: White House Ruin in Canyon de Chelly.

Two mountain ranges stretch across Navajoland. The Lukachukais make up the northern extension of the large Chuska range, stretching along the northern Arizona–New Mexico border. Chuska means "white spruce" and Lukachukai means "reeds extend white" in Navajo. With sand dunes at their feet, their peaks range from 7,500 to almost 10,000 feet in elevation and are covered with lakes, meadows, aspens, and willows. Cattle and sheep are brought to pasture there in the summer.

Navajo Mountain rises 10,388 feet above Lake Powell on the Arizona–Utah border. The mountain is sacred to the Navajos, who call it Naatsis'aan ("pollen mountain"). Navajo sandstone dominates the structure of the mountain and erodes easily into interesting shapes. Ponderosa pine, spruce, fir, and aspen trees populate the peak's upper elevations. Like most landforms on the reservation, the mountain is associated with a rich oral tradition that has been passed down through countless generations of Navajos.

Left: Cove Mesa Arch at sunrise.

Above: Sandstone cliffs have been eroded into faces reminiscent of Easter Island.

Below: Lupines bloom amidst sand dunes on the Navajo Reservation.

Navajo & Hopi Reservations

The Navajo Nation occupies over 27,000 square miles in northeastern Arizona, southern Utah, and northwestern New Mexico. With a population now surpassing 250,000, the Navajo Nation is both the largest and most populous reservation in the United States. Navajos descended from the Athapaskans of Canada, arriving in the Southwest as early as 1,000 years ago, with substantial numbers present by about 500 to 600 years ago. Influenced by Pueblo neighbors and Spanish colonists, Navajos became expert weavers and horsemen, while retaining their language and ceremonies. About two-thirds still live on ancestral lands and are engaged in cattle and sheep ranching, while many others have entered into professional occupations on and off the reservation. Navajo artisans are known for their silversmithing, sandpainting art, and varied weaving styles, some unique to specific locations.

In 1863 the U.S. government sent Colonel Kit Carson to round up the Navajos and lead them to the Bosque Redondo reservation (called Hweeldi, "place of suffering," by the Navajos) in New Mexico. Starting in January of 1864, the Navajos were forced to walk 400 miles without enough food or warm clothes. Many died on the terrible journey known as the Long Walk. After the government failed in its attempt to force the Navajos to succeed at agriculture in their new home, where conditions were terrible and food was scarce, the Navajos were allowed to return to their homelands four years later, once more on foot.

The smaller Hopi Reservation is completely surrounded by the Navajo Nation. The land is high and dry, and villages occupy the bases and tops of three steep mesas: First, Second, and Third Mesa. The sandstone cliffs of the mesas rise sharply above the reddish Moenkopi Formation typical of the plateau. Springs bubble up from underground aquifers, making the villages' agrarian lifestyle possible. The horizon around the mesas is marked by views of the San Francisco Peaks and the jagged silhouettes of volcanic features, used for centuries as a solar calendar.

Old Oraibi on Third Mesa (along with Acoma Pueblo in New Mexico) is considered the longest continuously inhabited settlement in the United States. Despite the efforts of missionaries to impose Christianity and Anglo-European culture on the Hopis, they have remained largely traditional, especially in their ceremonial practices. Hopi artisans are known for their pottery, basketry, weavings, kachina carvings, and distinctive overlay-style jewelry.

Left: A Hopi girl is dressed for a ceremony.
Above: Moki chief's blanket by Navajo weaver Barbara Teller Ornelas.

In the late 1800s Indian traders established posts throughout Indian Country, stocking goods like tools, coffee, and tobacco, and exchanging them with the Navajos for wool, pinyon nuts, or woven goods. The Navajos also created beautiful silver and turquoise jewelry that they could use as portable wealth. In times of need, they deposited their valuables with the trader, who would advance them cash for the items. When crops came in, sheep were shorn, or more blankets made, the owner would redeem his treasured jewelry. In many cases, the trader allowed the Navajos to "borrow" their jewelry out of pawn for special occasions.

When rail travel spurred tourist interest in the Southwest, traders encouraged tribal members to produce traditional crafts for sale. In 1878 John Lorenzo Hubbell established a post near Ganado, a Navajo town known for its weavings of red yarn and striking diamond designs. Hubbell Trading Post, now a national historic site, is the oldest continuously operating post on the Navajo Nation.

Two companies made their fortunes on railroad tourism and the Southwest's new romantic "land of enchantment" image. Native American crafts and cultures were a cornerstone of the Fred Harvey Company's partnership with the Santa Fe Railway. Harvey hotels and attractions at the Grand Canyon and elsewhere celebrated regional design, hosting weavers, silversmiths, potters, and dancers. In 1930 Flagstaff's Museum of Northern Arizona launched its first Hopi Craftsmen Exhibition. The annual summer festival is now the oldest Hopi art show in the world.

During World War II, the influence of Arizona's native cultures extended into an unexpected area. When the Imperial Japanese Army repeatedly broke American codes, the U.S. military turned to American Indian languages for help. New codes were based on Navajo, Hopi, and other languages, and messages were translated and transmitted by Code Talkers. The new codes proved to be unbreakable, and Arizona's Indians provided a priceless contribution to the war effort.

Top: Trader Bill Malone in the rug room of Hubbell Trading Post.
Middle: Bracelet by Hopi artist Dorothy Poleyma.
Bottom: Navajo Code Talkers.

Canyon de Chelly

Hidden away in the center of the Navajo Nation, Canyon de Chelly National Monument offers scenic overlooks, well-preserved prehistoric ruins, and a beautiful picture window into Navajo life. Carrying on family traditions, Navajos continue to herd sheep, raise horses, and cultivate crops on the valley floor between the sheer thousand-foot-high sandstone walls.

Canyon de Chelly and neighboring Canyon del Muerto contain impressive pictographs and petroglyphs from the Basketmaker, Pueblo, and Navajo periods, indicating the area's long history as shelter, home, and refuge. A pictograph above Standing Cow Ruin depicts a violent Spanish punitive expedition into the canyons in 1805. This canyon stronghold was also breeched by Kit Carson, marking his final assault on the Navajos before they were defeated and forced on the Long Walk to Bosque Redondo.

Spider Rock, a majestic sandstone spire, rises 800 feet from the floor of Canyon de Chelly. A Navajo sacred legend says that Spider Woman, the spirit who taught their people how to weave, lives at the top of Spider Rock, one of the highlights along South Rim Drive. North Rim Drive offers excellent views of Antelope Ruin, Ledge Ruin, and other dwellings built into caves in the red sandstone cliffs above the canyon floor between A.D. 1050 and 1300, when the Ancestral Puebloan culture was at its peak.

A steep trail (2.5 miles round trip) leads into the canyon to White House Ruin. To experience other canyon locales, visitors can hire Navajo guides or take one of the tours offered by historic Thunderbird Lodge, located at the junction of canyons del Muerto and de Chelly near Chinle.

Opposite: Spider Rock rises from the floor of Canyon de Chelly.

Top: Navajo pictograph of Spanish horsemen in Canyon del Muerto, depicting the Spanish invasion of the early 1800s.

Above: A Navajo hogon.

Monument Valley

Straddling the northern Arizona–Utah border on the Navajo Nation, Monument Valley Navajo Tribal Park contains more than a dozen majestic buttes and towers rising hundreds of feet in the air. Among the most famous formations are the Mittens, the Three Sisters, and Elephant Butte. The valley's vivid red color comes from iron oxide exposed in the weathered siltstone.

This landscape served as the backdrop for many American movies (especially those of director John Ford and his favorite star, John Wayne), creating the iconic image people around the world envision when they think of the American Southwest. Novelist Willa Cather compared Monument Valley's red sandstone formations to Gothic cathedrals, with wide vistas in between to allow the appreciation of nature's grand architecture. She wrote, "Elsewhere the sky is the roof of the world, but here the earth was the floor of the sky."

Antelope Canyon

Located on the Navajo Nation just a few miles east of Page, Arizona, Upper and Lower Antelope canyons are the most photogenic "slot canyons" in the Southwest. Slot canyons are usually formed by torrential floodwaters rushing through sedimentary deposits, creating fluted and sinuous walls. The magnificently sculpted canyons of Antelope Canyon Tribal Park are less than three feet wide in places, but more than 100 feet deep. From some locations above, the canyons appear to be a mere crack in the earth. Below, beams of sunshine enter at certain times of day, and the play of light and shadow turns the Navajo sandstone to shades of orange and purple.

Above: The beautifully sculpted rock of Antelope Canyon.

Left: The Mittens are the most recognizable formations in Monument Valley.

Petrified Forest & Painted Desert

Near the Colorado Plateau's southern edge, Petrified Forest National Park holds the world's largest and best collection of "permineralized" plant life. More than 200 million years ago, during the Late Triassic Period, ancient conifer trees washed down from eastern mountain ranges into sandy riverbeds, where they were buried in layers of gravelly sand and volcanic ash. As the logs decayed, carbonates and salts in water slowly replaced or enclosed living matter and eventually hardened into stone, over thousands of years. Iron and manganese oxides, carbon, silica (opal or chalcedony), and, rarely, chromium and cobalt replaced wood.

The ancient trees took on a glassy stone appearance with shades of red, yellow, black, brown, pink, green, and blue. The humid, tropical Late Triassic also supported a rich array of animal life, from invertebrate insects to early dinosaurs, whose fossilized remains are preserved in the colorful Chinle Formation.

In what we now call the Petrified Forest, water and wind shaped the landscape of sand dunes, grasslands, and badlands formed when clays filled with salts. Though annual rainfall measures less than ten inches, the land supports cottonwood, willow, juniper, shrubs like Mormon tea and four-wing saltbush, yuccas, prickly pear, cholla, and grasses. Animals such as rabbits, prairie dogs, quail, sandhill cranes, mule deer, bighorn sheep, and pronghorn antelope make their homes here.

Below: Petrified logs at last light in the Petrified Forest.

Opposite: The otherworldly colors and formations of the Painted Desert.

People also made their homes here, and more than 600 archaeological sites have been recorded within the park boundaries, which are undergoing expansion to enclose 218,533 acres. Ancient peoples valued petrified wood for its hard, smooth texture, useful for spear points and tools. The park's earliest human evidence comes from Paleo-Indian spear points dating to before 8000 B.C. The most populous time in the region was from A.D. 950 to 1200, when this area was at the edge of Mogollon and Ancestral Puebloan territory.

Petrified Forest National Park marks the eastern limits of the Painted Desert, which stretches more than 160 miles across northeastern Arizona to the rim of the Grand Canyon. It gets its name from the wide spectrum of colors in the siltstone, mudstone, and shale layers of the Chinle Formation, ranging from mauves, lavenders, and grays to vibrant pinks, oranges, and reds. The barren yet beautiful expanse of rolling hills and buttes was produced over millions of years by a combination of volcanoes, faults, and earthquakes interspersed with ocean flood sediment deposits that created the "multicolored layer cake" exposed today. Several highways and byways travel through the Painted Desert, much of which lies within the Navajo Nation. The Hopi Mesas rise above its northern edge, and it is bounded on the south by the Little Colorado River.

Little Colorado River

The Little Colorado River runs for 300 miles, from the White Mountains, through the Painted Desert, and finally rushes down into the Grand Canyon to join the Colorado River. Edward Abbey wrote, "Nowhere is water so beautiful as in the desert, for nowhere else is it so scarce." His words apply to many of Arizona's rivers and springs, but especially to the Little Colorado River, whose nature changes from a sparkling stream to a dry wash to a major tributary. People have depended on its flow for centuries.

In the 1870s Mormon colonists from Utah traveled up the Little Colorado River, establishing settlements in northeastern Arizona. Many of the early settlements were short-lived due to difficulties with crops, illness, and flooding, but Mormon families persevered and their descendants continue to live in historic towns—including St. John's, Springerville, and Eager—along the Little Colorado.

On its passage through the Navajo Nation, the river is dry for much of the year. But during the spring snowmelt from the White Mountains, the muddy brown waters tumble 185 feet over a ledge of sandstone at Grand Falls, a startling sight. At this remote location northeast of Flagstaff, the river cuts down the Colorado Plateau from the lower Moenkopi Formation (Triassic Period, 250 million years ago) through the top of the Permian Coconino Sandstone.

The Little Colorado continues its way toward the Grand Canyon, cutting a deep gorge on its final run. Near Cameron, the eastern gateway to Grand Canyon National Park, a Navajo Nation tribal park provides impressive views of the Little Colorado River Gorge. Further downstream, mineralized springs add travertine to the Little Colorado's waters, turning them turquoise before they join with the deep green of the Colorado River. ✳

Right: The Grand Falls at peak flow.

Below: The Little Colorado turns brilliant turquoise before it joins the Colorado River in the Grand Canyon.

Out West, the west of the mesas and the unpatented hills, there is more sky than any place in the world. It does not sit flatly on the rim of earth, but begins somewhere out in the space in which the earth is poised, hollows more, and is full of clean winey winds.

—MARY AUSTIN, *LAND OF LITTLE RAIN*

Desert Country

Arizona is the only state that includes three of North America's four major deserts: Sonoran, Mojave, and Chihuahuan. Even the fourth, the Great Basin Desert, is represented in the inner Grand Canyon, which hosts desertscrub typical of the Great Basin region. The Arizona Strip, north of the Grand Canyon, is also considered by some to be part of the Great Basin Desert.

Left: Organ pipe cactus. Above: Organ Pipe Cactus National Monument in full bloom.

Arizona's largest cities are in the Sonoran Desert, which covers 120,000 square miles in Arizona and California, and in the states of Sonora and Baja California in Mexico. The desert is home to 350,000 plant species, 500 bird species, 120 mammalian species, and countless invertebrates. Although it is the hottest of the North American deserts, a surprising number of plants thrive in the Sonoran Desert's harsh conditions. The desert abounds in mesquite and palo verde trees, as well as its signature columnar cactus, the saguaro.

Arizona's deserts have long challenged people to survive and thrive. The growth and decline of communities and civilizations have always been subject to the availability of water. The quest for water is a struggle even today, as growing metropolises demand an ever-greater supply. More than 80 percent of Arizona's residents call the desert cities of Phoenix and Tucson home. Water and modern transportation allowed these cities to grow. Like its feathered namesake, Phoenix "rose from the ashes" of the Hohokam civilization through the restoration of their ancient canals and the building of new ones. Tucson grew rapidly after the arrival of the Southern Pacific Railroad in 1880, and major highway systems created a healthy tourist economy throughout the state. No longer cut off by vast stretches of desert, people and products could move much more swiftly and easily across the state.

Hardly barren wastelands, Arizona's deserts host a great variety of plant and animal life, all of which have adapted to live in a land of little water and extreme temperatures.

Phoenix

In central Arizona, the Phoenix metropolitan area, known as the Valley of the Sun, sprawls across the desert that was once home to the ancient Hohokam civilization. In this land of contrasts, vast green lawns dotted with blue pools and surrounded by palm trees lie in the middle of an arid desert.

The arrival of affordable air-conditioning in the 1950s allowed the population to explode, and its growth hasn't slowed down since. Phoenix has all the amenities of a large urban area, with a wealth of restaurants, shopping, museums, and sports. March is an especially popular month to be in the Phoenix area, as numerous professional baseball teams converge in the Valley of the Sun for spring training. The mild months of winter and early spring are also popular times to enjoy golf as player or spectator on impossibly lush greens surrounded by saguaros.

The Heard Museum and Taliesin West are two great places to get a taste of history and art. The Heard Museum was founded in 1929 to house the Heard family's collection of American Indian art and artifacts. The Heard seeks to educate the public about the cultures and arts of native peoples, with an emphasis on the Southwest. It has grown into an internationally recognized modern museum, renowned for the quality of its collections.

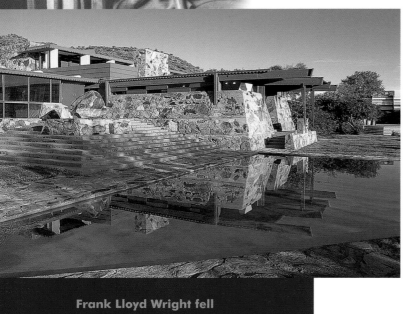

Frank Lloyd Wright fell in love with Arizona and built Taliesin West.

Told by his doctor that he could extend his life by wintering in Arizona instead of in frigid Wisconsin, famed American architect Frank Lloyd Wright began building Taliesin West in 1937. He selected 600 acres in the foothills of the McDowell Mountains near Scottsdale. The complex was inspired by, and harmonized with, its desert surroundings. It served as Wright's winter home, studio, and architecture school. The first Taliesin built by Wright was his Wisconsin home, where he died in 1959.

Those who want to learn about the flora and fauna of Arizona can do so without leaving the city. The Phoenix Zoo is the nation's largest privately owned, nonprofit zoo. Founded in 1962, it has become one of most popular attractions in the Phoenix area. The zoo, well known for its worldwide conservation efforts, houses animals in environments that replicate their natural habitats. It includes an Arizona Trail that exhibits animals native to the Sonoran Desert.

The world-class Desert Botanical Garden is home to 139 rare, threatened, and endangered desert plant species from around the world, with an emphasis on plants of the Southwest. It is known for its efforts in conservation, education, and research.

Top: Saguaros in Tonto National Forest.

Above: Bobcats can be found on the fringes of urban development, and also at the Phoenix Zoo.

*I was struck by the beauty of the desert,
by the dry, clear sun-filled air, by the stark
geometry of the mountains.*

—FRANK LLOYD WRIGHT

The Salt River, which gives life to the Valley of the Sun, is created by the merging of the White and Black Rivers in the White Mountains, and tumbles through Salt River Canyon before hitting the four reservoirs created by Roosevelt Dam. Past the dam, the Salt merges with the Verde River, but its flow is greatly diminished. The riverbed through the Phoenix area, which once supplied water to the Hohokams, is now dry except during rainy periods. A notable exception is Tempe's Town Lake, created by inflatable dams.

The Roosevelt Dam was completed in 1911 at the confluence of the Salt River and Tonto Creek, to combat drought and floods and support the growing population of Phoenix, then an agricultural community of about 20,000. A year later, Arizona became a state, and an image of Roosevelt Dam was included on the state seal. Roosevelt Lake is the first and largest of the reservoirs—which also include Saguaro, Canyon, and Apache lakes—created by the dam at the foot of Four Peaks.

Four Peaks rise from the south end of the Mazatzal Mountains, a range that runs roughly north-south through central Arizona. These hard peaks of quartzite, shale, and granite create a very distinctive silhouette visible from the Phoenix area. Ponderosa pine hugs the upper elevations. The Verde River runs along the range's west side, joining the Salt River on its run to the desert below.

Top: The Four Peaks are blanketed by snow in winter.

Above: Coulter's lupine blooms during spring.

Left: Canyon Lake is one of four reservoirs created by Roosevelt Dam.

Below: A Hohokam pot.

The Apache Trail, built to serve the dam construction, was striking enough to be publicized as a scenic route in a 1916 *Sunset* magazine article. The Apache Trail remains a scenic route today, winding along the Salt River and the Superstition Mountains, forming a loop that encloses the Superstition Wilderness, the legendary site of the Lost Dutchman Mine. The route also passes below Tonto National Monument, which preserves a pair of large cliff dwellings occupied by the Salado people from the 1200s until their abandonment in the early 1400s.

Along the Salt River in Phoenix lies a partially excavated ancient Hohokam village, the largest of many that lie beneath the modern metropolis. Called Pueblo Grande, it encompasses residential compounds, one large dwelling, hundreds of small houses, and several ancient ballcourts. At its peak in the 1300s, Pueblo Grande was located in the midst of a major canal system that irrigated extensive agricultural fields. The community was vacated in the 1400s when Hohokam society collapsed. Pueblo Grande Museum Archaeological Park preserves and interprets the site. Further south, halfway between Phoenix and Tucson, the Hohokams constructed massive, four-story-high Casa Grande of mud and wood. Casa Grande, now a national monument, was once surrounded by residential compounds and dwellings such as those at Pueblo Grande.

Tucson

Arizona's second-largest city lies in southern Arizona. Tucson, nicknamed the "Old Pueblo," is a mixture of old and new, with a population of half a million and growing. Tucson was Arizona's largest city until Phoenix surpassed it in the early 1900s. People are drawn to Tucson by the University of Arizona, five-star resorts and spas, golfing, and the scenic desert setting.

A beautiful drive through the Tucson Mountains brings you to the Arizona-Sonora Desert Museum, one of Arizona's best and most popular attractions. This private, nonprofit museum allows visitors to view animals of the Sonoran Desert in their natural setting, while walking through beautiful landscaping full of native plants. The museum is dedicated to supporting education, conservation, and research associated with the Sonoran Desert. Tucson Botanical Gardens and Tohono Chul Park, both located within the city, are also great places to view and learn about desert plants.

Tucson's oldest neighborhoods are surrounded by a modern metropolis. Barrio Histórico and El Presidio historic districts in downtown give a glimpse into Tucson's past through their 19th-century architecture.

Saguaro National Park is the world's best place to experience a saguaro "forest." Stately, statuesque, and oddly human-shaped, the saguaro is Arizona's icon and the largest cactus native to the United States. Nothing depicts Arizona's rare desert beauty quite like a lone saguaro silhouette at sunset or moonrise. It grows only in the Sonoran Desert of Arizona and the Mexican state of Sonora, with a few exceptions along the Colorado River in California. Saguaros often reach heights of 50 feet and weigh 80 pounds per foot. They may begin to grow arms at about 12 feet in height, or 40 to 80 years of age. Saguaros may live up to 200 years. From April through June, large white flowers decorate the tops of saguaros, followed by bursting red fruit, a favorite of white-winged doves and a traditional food of the Tohono O'odham Indians. The fragrant saguaro blossom is Arizona's state flower.

Originally created as a national monument in 1933, the 91,000-acre conservation area became a national park in 1994. The park is divided into two sections that lie on either side of Tucson—20 miles east of downtown, below the Rincon Mountains, and 15 miles west, along the Tucson Mountains. Approximately 60,000 acres of the east unit are designated wilderness area, and each unit has an interpretive visitors' center. The park gets its name from the large number of native saguaros, but many other cactus species, including barrel, cholla, and prickly pear thrive here as well.

Southwest of Tucson along the Mexican border, Organ Pipe Cactus National Monument is the only place in the United States where you can see large stands of the majestic organ pipe cactus, named for its many columnar six-inch-diameter arms that branch out close to the ground and reach a height of up to 26 feet. Organ pipes can live more than 150 years, and do not produce flowers until they are 35. The Tohono O'odham people, whose large reservation stretches north and east of the monument, traditionally used the fruits of organ pipe and saguaro cacti as summer food sources.

In 1976 the United Nations designated Organ Pipe Cactus National Monument as an International Biosphere Reserve. More than 500 plant species and desert animals flourish here despite the intense sun, extreme temperature ranges, and lack of rain in the 516-square-mile preserve.

Above: The Tucson Courthouse.

Opposite: Petroglyphs can be found among the saguaros at Saguaro National Park.

*The waste places of the earth,
the barren deserts, the tracts forsaken of men and
given over to loneliness, have a peculiar attraction of
their own. The weird solitude, the great silence, the
grim desolation, are the very things with which every
desert wanderer eventually falls in love.*

—JOHN C. VAN DYKE, *THE DESERT*, 1901

Bordering Organ Pipe in the west, Cabeza Prieta National Wildlife Refuge is the third-largest wildlife refuge in the lower 48 states. The refuge protects the endangered Sonoran pronghorn.

Forming Tucson's northern horizon are the Santa Catalina Mountains, named by Father Eusebio Kino in the late 1600s for Saint Catherine. The Tohono O'odham people call the same mountain range Babad Do'ag, or Frog Mountain. The Santa Catalinas tower above the city, giving Tucsonans an ever-changing panorama of rugged beauty. They may appear hidden by rain clouds, or white with snow, or shrouded in purple shadows at sunset. The steep rise in elevation and varied topography support a variety of plant and animal life, from Sonoran desertscrub in the foothills at 2,400 feet in elevation, to grassland in mid-elevations, to pine forest and finally fir forest at the summit of Mount Lemmon at 9,157 feet.

Sabino Canyon cuts into the southeast side of the Santa Catalinas. The canyon has been a scenic haven for picnickers and hikers since the 1870s. Sabino Creek flows continuously through all seasons, though its volume can change dramatically depending on the amount of rain and mountain snowmelt. Devastating flash floods can occur during the summer monsoon season. Tannin from the oak trees along the banks gives the creek its distinctive nut-brown color. Spectacular granite and gneiss cliffs tower hundreds of feet above the creek. In the 1930s, federal New Deal agencies built nine dams across the creek, creating inviting ponds and waterfalls for the enjoyment of canyon visitors.

South of Tucson, a natural wonder lies underground. Kartchner Caverns is a rare living, wet cave, with more than 90 percent of its limestone formations still growing. Though formed around 200,000 B.C., the cave was first discovered in 1974 by cavers Randy Tufts and Gary Tenen on Kartchner Ranch in the Whetstone Mountains near Benson. A sinkhole and a small blowhole were the only clues to the massive caverns below. Before publicizing their findings, Tufts and Tenen made sure the cave was protected as a state park. Delicate stalactites, massive columns, and "bird nests" of needle quartz are just a few of the highlights you may see on guided tours through the caverns. The park is open year-round, though the Big Room closes from April to September, when it serves as a nursery roost for nearly 1,000 mytosis bats.

Above: Sabino Canyon's trademark nut-brown water flows gently past trees in fall color.

Opposite: Organ Pipe National Monument bursts with color during spring, when wildflowers like the lupines and brittlebush shown here bloom.

Top and above right: Bisbee miners circa 1910, and the town of Bisbee today.

Above: Even now, Tombstone retains its Old West atmosphere.

Tombstone & Bisbee

Further into southern Arizona, you can walk right into the Wild West. In the late 1870s friends warned prospector Ed Schieffelin that all he would find in the mountains of southeastern Arizona, an Apache stronghold, would be his own tombstone. Instead he discovered silver and gold, and the boomtown of Tombstone sprang up.

The big mining strike brought a rough and greedy crowd, hoping to strike it rich. In 1881 the Earp brothers and Doc Holliday clashed with the Clantons and McLaurys—ranchers and alleged cattle rustlers—in the famous Gunfight at the O.K. Corral. The shoot-out left three dead and three wounded during a period of dangerous turmoil in southern Arizona. By 1930, Tombstone's boomtown population of 8,000 or more had dwindled to a mere 150 people, but the "Town Too Tough to Die" has found new life as a window into the legendary Wild West.

About 25 miles down the road from Tombstone, the quaint historic mining town of Bisbee hugs the slopes of the Mule Mountains. Bisbee's mines yielded silver, gold, and a variety of minerals, but the "Queen of the Copper Camps" is best known for copper and turquoise. Collectors prize Bisbee Blue turquoise for its startling blue color and reddish matrix.

Southeastern Sky Islands

The Chihuahuan Desert occupies southeastern Arizona, central and southern New Mexico, and west Texas, extending far into Mexico. At 140,000 square miles, it is the second-largest desert in North America. Due to its generally higher elevations (2,000 to 5,000 feet) Chihuahuan Desert temperatures are cooler than those of the Sonoran Desert, and it receives more rainfall. It may be the most biologically diverse—and most endangered—desert in the world. Many species of low shrubs, leaf succulents, and cacti grow here, but trees are rare.

Lack of trees does not seem to bother Arizona's wide variety of birds, especially in the Chihuahuan Desert. Of the 330 known species of hummingbirds, it's possible to find at least 15 of them in southeastern Arizona between late July and early September, more than any place else in the United States. These flashy fliers measure three to five inches long fully grown, flaunting an iridescent rainbow of plumage. Many of them mate in the springtime in Arizona, then winter in Mexico. One species, the rufous hummingbird, migrates up to 12,000 miles a year, the farthest of all U.S. hummingbirds. Rufous hummingbirds arrive in parts of Arizona with the monsoon, a fitting entrance for a feisty bird.

One of Arizona's most spectacular bird-watching events is "Wings Over Willcox," occurring in mid-January when thousands of big gray birds with red-spotted foreheads and six-foot wingspans flock to this valley lying on the edges of the Sonoran and Chihuahuan deserts. The majority of the world's 20,000 sandhill cranes nest in Idaho, with other sites in Wyoming, Montana, Utah, and Alberta. They arrive in Arizona, New Mexico, and northern Mexico sometime in October to enjoy the warm climate through February. The majority, an annual average of 8,000 to 12,000 cranes, choose the Sulphur Springs Valley as their winter home. The best place to view the cranes is around the Willcox Playa, a dry lakebed a few miles south of the town of Willcox.

Hundreds of other birds also flock to the "sky islands," where the Sonoran and Chihuahuan deserts meet the Sierra Madrean and Rocky Mountain communities of higher elevations. Thousands of avian ecotourists travel to these mountains from all parts of the globe to catch a rare glimpse of the brightly colored scarlet-breasted elegant trogon (a relative of Guatemala's quetzal), which spends part of the year in the sky islands. Southeastern Arizona's mountains host a great diversity of other wildlife as well. Four species of skunks—striped, spotted, hooded, and hog-nosed—coexist on the sky islands and nowhere else in the world.

Sandhill cranes (above), broad-tailed hummingbirds (left), elegant trogans (below left), and acorn woodpeckers (below right) are some of the many species of birds that can be found in the Sky Islands of southeastern Arizona.

Above: Southern dogface butterfly near Fort Huachuca.

Right: Hoodoos are unique features of Chiricahua National Monument.

In the southeastern corner of Arizona, the Chiricahua Mountains' high peaks of uplifted rhyolite were once the home of central Chiricahua Apaches. They called the mountains the "Land of Standing Up Rocks," for the extraordinary rock formations (hoodoos) created by erosion. Just north of Chiricahua National Monument, Fort Bowie National Historic Site is cradled strategically in Apache Pass. The fort, established in 1862, played a key role in the Apache conflicts that lasted throughout the final half of the 19th century. Cochise, chief of the Chiricahuas in the mid-1800s, fought fiercely against the Mexicans but kept peace with U.S. citizens until he was falsely accused of kidnapping, which increased hostilities. Finally, in 1872 a treaty was negotiated between Cochise and the United States, but after his death a few years later, the U.S. government broke the terms of the treaty, and new leadership among the Apaches, including Geronimo, renewed the fight. Never a chief but always a leader, Geronimo was an Apache warrior and medicine man. He and his warriors had many conflicts with U.S. forces led by General George Crook and later General Nelson A. Miles. Geronimo and his small band of Chiricahuas held off thousands of U.S. and Mexican troops until their final surrender in 1886. The restive Chiricahua Apaches were confined first in Florida, then in Oklahoma, and later some were allowed to move to the Mescalero reservation in New Mexico. They never returned to their own lands.

Like many other places in Arizona, the former Apache lands have a rugged yet bountiful beauty. West of the Chiricahuas, the Huachuca Mountains rise against Arizona's border with Mexico. Peaks are topped by aspen and maple, while grassy hills make up the lower elevations. Canyons cut into the range's east side, offering varied habitats. Here, the San Pedro River flows north from Mexico, providing a migratory corridor for hundreds of bird species and a number of other animals. The San Pedro is one of the few free-flowing, undammed rivers in the Southwest. Cottonwoods and willows line its banks, creating a band of green through the desert.

In southern Arizona, the past is never far away. Near present-day Sierra Vista, Fort Huachuca was established in the Huachuca Mountains in 1877 to deal with continuing Apache raids into Mexico. Today, it is a National Historic Landmark as well as the only active military post that traces its roots to the Apache Wars. After the Civil War, the U.S. Army organized four regiments of black soldiers, many of them former slaves. The Tenth Cavalry "Buffalo Soldiers" were stationed at Fort Huachuca, protecting settlers and towns against Indian attacks, guarding the U.S.–Mexico border, and serving in the Spanish–American War. Twenty-three Buffalo Soldiers were awarded the Medal of Honor, the nation's most prestigious award for bravery. The fort's history museum, housed in an adobe-and-stone building that once served as post chapel, honors their legacy.

I was born on the prairies where the wind blew free and there was nothing to break the light of the sun. I was born where there were no enclosures.

—GERONOMO

Banded rock rattlesnakes inhabit the land that Geronimo (top) and the Chiricahua Apaches once called home.

Yuma

Arizona's third-largest metropolitan area has grown along the Colorado River. Health seekers, vacationers, retirees, and winter visitors (known locally as "snow birds") all flock to Yuma, one of the sunniest spots in the nation. The combination of sun, fertile river-bottom soil, and water makes the area an agricultural leader in citrus and cotton, as well as winter vegetables such as broccoli, cauliflower, and lettuce. Yuma's other-worldly desert was not only ideal for World War II military training, but also the perfect spot to shoot scenes for *Star Wars* movies.

Arizona's western border—and much of its history—is defined by the mighty Colorado River. One of the largest watercourses west of the Mississippi, it flows through five states, from the snow-clad Rocky Mountains through rugged canyons and three vast deserts, to the Gulf of California. It is approximately 1,450 miles long, running off the Rocky Mountains' western slope from northern Colorado to the desert just south of Yuma, Arizona. Its depth ranges from 6 to 100 feet as it drops from 9,000 feet to sea level on its journey through the Southwest. The Colorado travels through Arches and Canyonlands national parks in Utah before reaching Lake Powell, formed by the Glen Canyon Dam. There the water loses the red silted murkiness it was named for and becomes clear and cold as it heads for the Grand Canyon. West of the Grand Canyon the river turns abruptly southward into the Mojave Desert as it enters Lake Mead, formed by Hoover Dam, the massive water and power supplier for Las Vegas and southern California.

The Bill Williams River flows into the Colorado River near Yuma.

Along the California–Arizona border, four additional dams divert water for agricultural irrigation and recreation. The reservoirs hold 34 million acre-feet of water. Along the border, the Colorado River ranges in width from 700 to 2,500 feet and from 8 to 100 feet in depth.

Further south, the Colorado leaves the Mojave Desert and enters the Sonoran Desert. By the time it joins the Gila River at Yuma, its channel is bedded in concrete flood-control embankments. Once creating a vast delta at its entrance into the Gulf of California (or Sea of Cortez), the Colorado is now more of a trickle through plains of silt, struggling to reach the sea. Though the mighty Colorado has been tamed, it continues to support important riparian habitat in areas like Topock Gorge and Havasu, Cibola, and Imperial national wildlife refuges.

The Colorado River played an important part in Arizona's prehistory and history. Once an important travel corridor for the prehistoric Patayan people, later a gateway to California's gold fields via Yuma Crossing, the river currently supplies water to more than half of Arizona through the giant Central Arizona Project canal system, completed in 1994. The Cocopah, Quechan, Chemehuevi, and Mohave Indian tribes who historically lived along the Colorado River now occupy four reservations in the desert lands along the river. Agriculture, tourism, and water rights are important parts of the Colorado River tribes' economies.

Sixty miles north of Yuma and 15 miles east of the Colorado River, the volcanic Kofa Mountains stand in stark contrast between the barren desert and life-giving river. Kofa National Wildlife Refuge protects some of the unique flora and fauna of western Arizona. Kofa is simply "K of A"—an abbreviation for the King of Arizona gold mine, discovered in 1896. The jagged mountains rear up off the desert floor abruptly with no rolling hills in between, a steep climb from sea level to more than 4,000 feet in a few short miles. Hundreds of desert bighorn sheep inhabit these mountains, surviving on five inches of annual rainfall that allows for sparse plant life of cacti and creosote and—surprisingly—California fan palms, Arizona's only variety of the well-known oasis tree. There is no water source in these mountains except for natural *tinajas* (small pools that catch rain water in rocky hollows) and manmade tanks.

Top: Sand dunes like these are unique to the Yuma area in Arizona.

Above: California fan palms in Kofa National Wildlife Refuge are the only palms native to the state.

Lake Havasu

The Mojave Desert lies between the Sonoran Desert to the south and the Great Basin Desert to the north. Two-thirds of it occupies southeastern California, with the remaining third in southern Nevada and northwestern Arizona along the Colorado River. At approximately 25,000 square miles, it is the smallest of the three Arizona deserts. The Mojave is generally cooler and drier than the Sonoran Desert, receiving an average of only five inches of annual rainfall. Hard freezes are common in winter, while lower elevations can experience summer temperatures that soar above 100 degrees F.

London Bridge is the second-most popular attraction in Arizona, after the Grand Canyon.

Opposite: Boaters at sunset on Lake Havasu.

Mojave vegetation is predominantly shrub species, with few succulents, cacti, or trees. Elevations of 3,000 to 6,000 feet support the Mojave's most common plant, the Joshua tree. Mormon pioneers so named this species—the largest of the yuccas and a member of the lily family—because it reminded them of the prophet Joshua waving them on to the Promised Land.

In the middle of the Mojave Desert, the Parker Dam spans the Colorado River in northern Arizona. Known as the "deepest dam in the world," three-quarters of its 320-foot-height is below the original riverbed. Like Hoover Dam, it provides a great deal of water and electric power for the state of California.

Parker Dam was completed in 1938, forming beautiful Lake Havasu, a Havasupai word meaning "blue water." Chainsaw and motorboat magnate Robert McCulloch began testing his engines here in the 1950s, and created Lake Havasu City along the lake's southern shore in 1964. McCulloch gained international attention when he purchased and dismantled the London Bridge for $2.46 million in 1968, and reconstructed it across the Colorado River in the center of town. The bridge, constructed in 1824 to replace earlier London bridges at the same location dating back to 1100 A.D., is considered the second-most-popular attraction in Arizona, after the Grand Canyon.

Lake Havasu attracts 3.5 million visitors each year for recreational fishing and boating. Speedboats shoot white plumes of water 20 feet into the air along the Colorado River from Parker to Lake Havasu, towing water-skiers almost year-round in the hot, sunny climate that attracts water-sport fans from all over, especially during spring break. Even when it's 118 (degrees F) in the shade (and there isn't any shade), speeding across the cool blue water proves that Arizona's "dry heat" isn't so bad. ☀

Above: A red-tailed hawk flies over tufa columns in Chiricahua National Monument. Below: A golden mariposa blooms in Petrified Forest National Park.

Resources & Suggested Reading

Aleshire, Peter. *Desert Rivers: From Lush Headwaters to Sonoran Sands.* Phoenix: Arizona Highways Books, 2006.

Arizona Highways. *Arizona Hiking: Urban Trails, Easy Paths & Overnight Treks.* Phoenix: Arizona Highways Books, 2004.

Broyles, Bill. *Our Sonoran Desert.* Tucson: Rio Nuevo Publishers, 2003.

Bryant, Kathleen. *Sedona: Treasure of the Southwest.* Flagstaff: Northland Publishing, 2002.

Cheek, Lawrence W. *Frank Lloyd Wright in Arizona.* Tucson: Rio Nuevo Publishers, 2006.

———. *The Navajo Long Walk.* Tucson: Rio Nuevo Publishers, 2004.

Chronic, Halka. *Roadside Geology of Arizona.* Missoula, MT: Mountain Press Publishing Company, 1983.

Crutchfield, James A. *It Happened in Arizona: Remarkable Events that Shaped History.* Guilford, CT: Globe Pequot Press, 2010.

Economic Development Research Program, University of Arizona. http://edrp.arid.arizona.edu/tribes.html

Farmer, Jared. *Glen Canyon Dammed: Inventing Lake Powell & the Canyon Country.* Tucson: University of Arizona Press, 1999.

Hall, Sharlot. *Poems of a Ranch Woman.* Prescott: Sharlot Hall Museum Press, 1989.

Houk, Rose. *The Mountains Know Arizona: Images of the Land and Stories of Its People.* Phoenix: Arizona Highways Books, 2003.

Hull, Tim. *Moon Guides: Arizona.* Berkeley: Avalon Travel, 2008.

Humphreys, Anna, and Susan Lowell. *Saguaro: The Desert Giant.* Tucson: Rio Nuevo Publishers, 2002.

Gattuso, John. *Insight Guides: Arizona & the Grand Canyon.* Singapore: APA Publications, 2009.

Jones, Anne Trinkle. *Stalking the Past: Prehistory at the Petrified Forest.* Petrified Forest National Park: Petrified Forest Museum Association, 1993.

Lamberton, Ken. *Chiricahua Mountains: Bridging the Borders of Wilderness.* Tucson: University of Arizona Press, 2003.

Lucchitta, Ivo. *Hiking Arizona's Geology.* Seattle: The Mountaineers Books, 2001.

Nickens, Paul, and Kathleen Nickens. *Native Americans of Arizona.* Charleston, SC: Arcadia Publishing, 2007.

Niethammer, Carolyn. *West of Paradise: Exploring Southeastern Arizona.* Tucson: Rio Nuevo Publishers, 2003.

Noble, David Grant. *Ancient Ruins of the Southwest: An Archaeological Guide.* Flagstaff: Northland Publishing, 2000.

Plog, Stephen. *Ancient Peoples of the American Southwest, 2nd ed.* London: Thames & Hudson, 2008.

Reid, Jefferson, and Stephanie Whittlesey. *The Archaeology of Ancient Arizona.* Tucson: The University of Arizona Press, 1997.

Rio Nuevo Publishers. *The Grand Canyon: From Rim to River.* Tucson: Rio Nuevo Publishers, 2010.

Sheridan, Thomas E. *Arizona: A History.* Tucson: The University of Arizona Press, 1995.

Silas, Anna. *Journey to Hopi Land.* Tucson: Rio Nuevo Publishers, 2006.

Trimble, Marshall. *Roadside History of Arizona, 2nd ed.* Missoula, MT: Mountain Press Publishing Company, 2004.

———. *Arizona: A Calvacade of History, rev. ed.* Tucson: Rio Nuevo Publishers, 2003.